STRIKE ANYWHERE

Michael Lista

STRIKE
ANYWHERE

Essays, Reviews
& Other Arsons

The Porcupine's Quill

Library and Archives Canada Cataloguing in Publication

Lista, Michael, 1983–, author
    Strike anywhere : essays, reviews & other arsons / Michael Lista.

ISBN 978-0-88984-392-9 (paperback)

    1. Canadian poetry (English)—20th century—History and
criticism. 2. Canadian poetry (English)—21st century—History and
criticism. 3. American poetry—20th century—History and criticism.
4. American poetry—21st century—History and criticism. I. Title.

PS8155.L58 2016   C811'.5409   C2016-902395-8

Published by The Porcupine's Quill, 68 Main Street,
PO Box 160, Erin, Ontario NOB 1TO. http://porcupinesquill.ca

Represented in Canada by Canadian Manda.
Trade orders are available from University of Toronto Press.

We acknowledge the support of the Ontario Arts Council and
the Canada Council for the Arts for our publishing program.
The financial support of the Government of Canada through
the Canada Book Fund is also gratefully acknowledged.

for Madeleine

TABLE OF CONTENTS

INTRODUCTION

When I was asked to collect some of my journalism from the last few years, I remembered what Geoff Dyer said about this sort of miscellany, that it made for 'a pretty low form of book, barely a book at all.' On the other hand, lots of these essays and reviews got me into all kinds of fire and brimstone type shit, and helped put the torch to what had been, in the halcyon days before my self-immolation, the beginning of a nice little career in Canadian letters. Eventually I thought it might be fun to collate all my arsons into one pile, so that by its light you—and I—could see where it all went wrong.

I used to have it pretty good. After Anansi published my first book of poems, I accepted an offer to work as a columnist for the *National Post*, writing a column on essentially whatever I wanted, so long as it had something to do with poetry. Not long after that, I was hired as the poetry editor for *The Walrus*, the most widely circulated Canadian magazine that still publishes poetry. I appreciated how funny it was too: I had dropped out of college, and at twenty-six was being mailed steady paycheques to do homework for money.

All I needed to do was not fuck it up, which, naturally, I did with characteristic haste, and, I'd like to think, style. The truth was that I didn't deserve those gigs when I got them. I landed them because I'd just published a book of poems that some people were talking about, and capitalized on the attention by making the right friends in the Toronto literary and journalism scenes. With the column, I didn't know what I was doing. There were a bunch of poetry critics who deserved the job before I did, but I was drinking with the right people and they weren't.

More importantly, those critics had disqualified themselves from a gig like mine because they'd made the mistake of having already distinguished themselves at theirs. They couldn't be literary critics in a major Canadian newspaper because they were literary critics. There was an unspoken understanding that book reviewers in major newspapers were expected to produce copy that was essentially service journalism, defanged consumer reports intended for the sort of reader who, on a whim, might buy a book on an outing to the mall for a new handbag or belt.

And so in my first few columns, I dutifully toed the party line, and wrote shallow book reviews in which the fathoms of my mixed feelings were left utterly unsounded. I got good at spinning candied empty calories, like when I gushed that Canada was in a golden age of poetry, which was just the sort of saccharine, confected falsehood that nearly everyone who read me had a sweet tooth for. Those early columns didn't deserve their first lives, never mind a belated second one here.

But after rushing down the street to the newsstand on the Saturday mornings when my column would run, and admiring myself in the empty Presse Internationale—which was soon to close for good—I couldn't help but notice the discrepancy between the sort of work I was filing, and the criticism of the writers I most admired—George Orwell, Gore Vidal, Helen Vendler, Philip Larkin, Christopher Hitchens, Janet Malcolm, Carmine Starnino, Mary Kinzie, Jason Guriel, Clive James, Renata Adler, Christian Wiman and others. Wiman wrote that if you're a book reviewer who loves most of the poetry that comes across your desk, you're either really lucky, or really stupid.

And so after only a few months, I was face to face with the dilemma of the Canadian poet-critic: bullshit your way to the top, or realtalk your way to the bottom. I knew lots of people in the scene who had parlayed their column inches and entry-level editorial jobs into some pretty cushy gigs, and the temptation to accept the keys to the kingdom, which were on offer for the low price of my conscience, was very real indeed. And you don't get to fulminate in the white-shoe real estate for long before the insular, interbred village of Canadian poets pulls out the pitchforks, feathers and tar.

In other words, I had to decide whether or not I would continue to let poetry be useful to me. It had been the only thing that rescued me from the couch to which I'd resigned myself after the novel I'd dropped out of college to finish collapsed under the weight of its own wretchedness. Poetry had afforded me a modicum of recognition, a modest living and the imprimatur of well-heeled media organs. But the exigencies of the new life it had given me meant that I could be either a poetry critic, or the kind of poetry critic I wanted to be, but not both.

So, against my better judgement, I filed my first skeptical review, and passed judgement on the latest collection of poems by a CanLit patron saint, the former Catholic priest Tim Lilburn. The book, *Assiniboia*, ostensibly about Louis Riel and his provisional government, embodied so much of what I despised about huge swaths of Canadian poetry: a conspicuous environmentalism that masked a deep-seated misanthropy; a vain self-regard of its own social consciousness; diction and cadences that were more noisy than musical. When it was funny, it was only ever by accident, like when Lilburn swoons with 'Copernican weightlessness', and in a mixed metaphor straight out of a nightmare game of Twister, 'lean(s) under it/to find the nipple of rest.' The jacket copy, when it bothered to make sense, was so grandiose as to give the impression that if the book could be ground down and snorted, it would be a panacea, but it wouldn't get you high: 'In *Assiniboia*, Tim Lilburn's wholesale attempt to resituate the root of human singing deep in the body's core amounts to a resuscitation of singing itself.' In other words: Lilburn's book, like so much contemporary poetry, was policy advocacy, social work and medicine at once; it was everything except fun. For the first time I let myself wonder aloud: are there literate adults who actually dig this?

Yes, it turns out. And as I learned shortly after the review was published, they're in possession of social media accounts. People were furious with me, and not just substantively; by writing a 'negative review', as the country's only national poetry columnist, I was somehow making a category error. Maybe I was naïve, but I didn't think I was saying anything particularly controversial. William Logan's sentence-long survey of the last half-millennium of poetry seemed axiomatic: 'Let's face it, the vast majority of books published since Gutenberg invented his movable type and Caxton inked up his press in England have possessed few virtues and all too many flaws.' And poetry for me was just one wavelength on the contiguous spectrum of contemporary arts and culture. I had, after all, published in the *Post's* Arts section, next to record and TV reviews, which were often skeptical and censorious. If a new hip-hop mixtape or web-series had lines as hilariously self-serious as *Assiniboia's*— like 'fog/Goatishly circling and sniffing/The anus of Mount Baldy'—most critics would make spectacular hay of it, and most discerning readers would get a kick out of the ensuing copy.

But those reviewers have what a Canadian literary critic doesn't: an independent readership. The only people who read my columns were in all likeliness Canadian writers, editors, publishers, or publicists themselves. They were the very people who were using poetry as raw material for their careers. And so when I criticized the swollen bloviating of *Assiniboia's* jacket bumph, it turned out that I was slagging the guy who wrote it,

Ken Babstock, my erstwhile friend, the most beloved poet of his generation, and the poetry editor of the House of Anansi, which published my first book. With every skeptical review I filed over the next few years, I was pissing off a handful of interconnected people, and there were only so many handfuls. I was also rapidly depleting my usefulness to the people in our puddle-sized ecosystem.

Because Canadian literary types are as self-righteous as they are thin-skinned, the backlash to my criticism became more histrionic and more panicked with each review I filed. When a poet noticed that I had reviewed more men than women in one calendar year, she surmised that I was sexist. When I aired my mixed feelings about Aisha Sasha John's second book—in a review in which, by the way, I call her brilliant—I was called a racist on Twitter by a white dude with a PhD. During an exchange with the tenured philosopher and poet Jan Zwicky in the pages of the *Post* in which I defend skeptical reviews, Zwicky likened them to rape:

Some people write negative reviews because they enjoy feeling hatred; they find it erotically satisfying. That the writing of viciously negative reviews can satisfy sadistic impulses does not surprise me; but it is a weakness of my essay that I failed to discuss such satisfaction as a conscious motive. Is it, in fact, a good moral defence of the practice of negative reviewing? No. In sexual encounters, our culture condones sadistic behaviour only between consenting adults. I see no reason to think that our standards should be different for critics and the critiqued.

The good professor may have been overstating her case just a bit, but she was right that I was having fun. I never thought I'd get the chance to rehash Milton's *Areopagitica* in a national newspaper in the twenty-first century, but now a doctor of philosophy had presented the happy opportunity. The scrutiny and incredulity with which I knew my more controversial pieces would be received sharpened my prose, so by being a more hated writer, I was becoming a better one. I was like that evil black planet in *Fifth Element* that expanded when it was attacked. And I took it as a kind of compliment that the only ripostes my own critics could offer in response were of the *ad hominem* variety; it meant my reputation was a preferable target for a counterattack than my arguments, the latter of which I cared about more anyway.

But my editor at the *Post* himself got a lot of hate mail about my columns, from writers, editors, publishers and advertisers. When he moved to another newspaper, I had a sense that the incoming editor at the *Post* was going to kill my column (she did), and so asked if he'd consider moving it over with him. He shot me a look of pity. He was tired of defending me and was probably right to worry that I might not just be imperilling my own career, but his too. And so as soon as I had finally earned my job as a Canadian literary critic, I had simultaneously disqualified myself from it.

Poetry is worth a damn because it isn't good for anything. It doesn't do well under the strain of being therapy, social advocacy, linguistic research, hagiography or gospel. Poetry buckles under the weight of occasion, like weddings and funerals, when most of us most frequently turn to it for guidance and consolation. It's almost always at its lowest when it presumes itself to be high art. And yet nearly everyone in the Canadian literary ecosystem is interested primarily in poetry's utility—how it can redress injustice, solve the problems of language's incommunicability and advance our careers.

John Keats bemoaned the faintest whiff of utility in a poem, writing that 'we hate poetry that has a palpable design upon us.' Nearly every fault these essays register, from the verses of Don McKay to the music of Leonard Cohen to presidential inaugural poems to the pretensions of the *avant garde* to the moral quandary of the Griffin Prize, arises from people taking poetry too seriously, which is to say not seriously enough. It's the critic's job to defend poetry from those who would inflate its value, like the central banker responsible for the currency of a banana republic.

In other words, the sooner a poet accepts Auden's declaration that 'poetry makes nothing happen', the sooner her poems will start to do something. Why? Because a poem with pretensions of utility assumes that its subject matter is the only reason its language matters, when in fact language is the only thing of value a poem can offer.

But if poems are priceless precisely because they're worthless, there's little incentive for the critic to admit that sort of thing in public. It's much more advantageous to her career in Canada to treat the poem itself as useful—breaking new linguistic ground, advocating for righteous public policy, etc.

That isn't to say that there aren't good Canadian poems. It's just impossible to talk about what's good about Canadian poetry without first talking about what's bad. So: there's both too little Canadian poetry and too much. Too little in the sense that our first decent English-speaking poet, E.J. Pratt, wasn't born until 1884, and our first great one, A.M. Klein, tarried until 1909. And too much? Because to make up for lost time, beginning in the 1950s, federal, provincial and municipal granting agencies started disbursing taxpayer dollars to Canadian writers and publishers. It suddenly became easier to publish a book of poems here than anywhere else in the world. This coincided with a wave of literary nationalism that made American and British influences suspect. The biggest beneficiary of this mindset was arguably Al Purdy. Imagine a kind of down-market D.H. Lawrence, mixed with the worst of Charles Bukowski. If Purdy didn't represent what we were, he embodied what we wanted to be: an early formalist who broke the shackles of foreign traditions to embrace an unpretentious, rural vernacular—a voice that poet and critic David Solway called 'Standard Average Canadian'. Solway goes on to say that Purdy is an enduring Canadian poet not because he sounded different than every other poet, but because he showed us how to all sound the same, which is what Canadians secretly desire.

Of course, Purdy's imitators and heirs wouldn't have ruled the roost for so long if our critics hadn't cooperated. Northrop Frye argued that since Canada hadn't yet produced a major writer, Canadian literature should never be read evaluatively, only thematically. 'If evaluation is one's guiding principle,' Frye wrote in 1965, 'criticism of Canadian literature would become only a debunking project, leaving it a poor naked alouette plucked of every feather of decency and dignity.' (An alouette is a songbird—a lark—in a popular Canadian nursery rhyme, which gets defeathered for waking a sleeping provincial with its provincial music.) This had the unintended consequence of making a mandate out of our mistakes, giving the legions of well-funded, inward-looking Canadian poets the permission they needed to succeed at being second rate. (In some quarters, it was a sign of one's authenticity to be ignored abroad.) One of our better novelists, Mordecai Richler, had a biting encomium for the kind of career that was now possible: he said you could be 'world-famous in Canada'. Canadian poets are the ketchup chips of the literary world; they're huge here, and don't exist anywhere else.

As with all of our exports, our best poets are incidentally, not essentially, Canadian—like Justin Bieber or basketball. If there's anything that binds them together besides excellence, it very well may be a shared mistrust of Canadian nationalism—or even of Canadianness itself—and an ambition to escape the inertia of its orbit. One of our finest poets, Daryl Hine—whose sonnet sequence about the neighbourhoods of Paris, 'Arrondissements', is a masterpiece—had this to say about how his expatriation began: 'I compensated for my lack of a B.A. (which I thought correctly that I should never need) by taking a Ph.D. at the University of Chicago, and instead of the work in a bookshop that I had been offered in Montreal, found myself editor of *Poetry*.' Today Hine's sculpted, Apollonian stanzas are still a niche taste among Canadian poets. If they'd had their way, he'd have stayed at the bookstore where he belonged. It's a Canadian fate.

And so it should come as no surprise that many of our most interesting poets are either immigrants (Irving Layton, A.M. Klein, Elise Partridge, Eric Ormsby, John Thompson, Ricardo Sternberg) or expatriates (Daryl Hine, P.K. Page, Anne Carson, Alexandra Oliver). For the same reason that our fantasy of a Canadian shibboleth ended up manifesting as a kind of couch-potato lingua franca, our most daring poets are linguistic high flyers precisely because they're frequent flyers. Layton took us to Greece, Partridge and Ormsby to Florida, Sternberg and Page to Brazil, Oliver to Scheveningen Beach in the Netherlands. More and more, those journeys are imaginary journeys, the inward and backward odysseys into literature and myth itself that Amanda Jernigan and Anne Carson and James Pollock have led us through. When they return with their poems, Standard Average Canadian simply won't do to convey the mystery and romance of the foreign. Instead, the language is torqued, decorous, ambitious and lexically tricked out with exotic, scientific, technical and archaic vocabularies. Karen Solie's 'Thrasher' (first published in *Modern and Normal*, Brick Books, 2005) pegs the new Canadian poet not as a poor naked alouette, but as another bird, a kind of magpie with a gift for mimicry, and if you try to pluck it, you'll get an earful:

> Yellow-legs ekes lower at nightfall to a stick nest
> brambled in the shade-kill, doing for himself, deft
>
> as a badger in a hammock. Mornings, toeing wracked heights
> of the cottonwood, he flaps his brown flag above alkaline
>
> slough beds, over plowlands attesting
> to the back and forth of work, their brown degrees
>
> scriven by road allowance cut at right angles through shriven
> weeds, fenceposts bracketing brown rut lines slantwise
>
> in relief. In relief at the topmost, he mimics domestic, migrant,
> spaniel, spring peepers, quacks, urks, and gurgles akin
>
> to a four-stroke in heavy water. He's slightly
>
> off. None respond. His own call is the vinyl scratch
> between tracks, a splice point. He was hatched
>
> that way, ferruginous, a wet transistor
> clacking from the egg in which he had lain curled

as an ear with an itch inside. He carries on
like AM radio. Like a prison rodeo. Recounts loser
baseball teams, jerry-riggers, part-timers, those paid in scrip,
anyone who has come out of retirement once

too often. He is playbacks, do-overs, repeats, repeats
the world's clamorous list, makes it his, replete,

and fledges from persistence what he is.

Here is what makes Canadian poets interesting: when we steal the whole world for ourselves, and sing it in all its useless complexity. And in our travels we've also rediscovered the literary inheritance that for so long we'd been told was a poisoned dowry (in the Solie we can hear the parrotings of everyone from Hopkins to Raymond Chandler). Like the kid raised on microwaveable fare who grows up to be a slow-food chef, Canadians are uniquely positioned at the moment—the way Derek Walcott was decades ago—to reinvigorate and reinterpret the traditional formal repertoire because we've been estranged from it for so long. Notice how in 'Thrasher', the bird becomes more himself as he becomes more larcenous, and that the Thrasher's final theft is form, Solie's feminine rhyming couplet (repeats/replete) glissanding into the iambic pentameter of the closing line. As Robert Frost said of Edwin Arlington Robinson, we've rediscovered 'the old fashioned way to be new'.

What our best poets share is a kind of renaissance sensibility. They've kicked at the dirt long enough to discover that there's another world buried under this one. We've set out beyond our borders, with our flag stitched to our backpack, and found the world an altogether more welcoming and nourishing place than we'd been warned it was. What the nationalists somehow overlooked was that to be distrustful of the foreign is the very essence of provincialism. Today, if our poets keep a lower profile than some of our splashier British and American cousins—well that's just like us. But we're secretly Canadian among them, like so many Seth Rogans and telephones.

———————

There are essentially three ways to write about art: as an academic study, as service journalism, and as self-reporting. As the infamous publisher Samuel Roth put it: 'I was too much in love with books to make a good student,' so I couldn't write like an academic. I never saw the point of trying to sell people books of poems in newspapers and magazines, so the service journalism approach was out. These essays are self-reporting, my only option. *Strike Anywhere* was written over about five years, and reading through it now I realize that it's essentially a memoir composed in slow motion, by accident, and only about one thing. One of my most vociferous and assholic critics used to call my column—which was named On Poetry—'On Myself'. He'd tweet that mercilessly, and intended it to wound, but it didn't; he was absolutely right.

In other words, *Strike Anywhere* can be read as a piece of investigative reporting into what Marianne Moore's 'perfect contempt' for poetry actually is, and what the genuine place it leads you to might look like (hint: it's the one without all the fancy jobs). Of course it's different for everyone—this is mine. But to pretend that poetry can be read any meaningful way *except* personally strikes me as fantastically naïve and quaint. I ached for something in poems that can only be found rarely and exists in the particular, like love (I know what it means to love this person, but not 'people', just as I know what it means to love that poem, but not 'poetry'). Pretending you can love every poem that comes across your desk is like pretending you can marry the whole world. And like loving, by reading other people, I discovered who I was.

As a result, I get called one word more than any other: 'polarizing'. It follows me around like a shadow, a big flat figure with two dimensions and no features. I happen to think that a critic's job is to file critically and with wit and flare about the books and ideas we take for granted, regardless of the personal cost. Only in Canada does that make you polarizing; everywhere else it simply makes you competent. I've also, as I think this book shows, spent just as much time shining a light on writers as I have casting shade. But no one remembers your raves; only your scorched pans stick.

And of course this is Canada, about whose well-behaved inhabitants Northrop Frye said: we're just Americans who rejected the revolution. We like to imagine ourselves as progressive, and maybe here and there we are, but constitutionally we're still Loyalists, in politics and in poetry both, and we hate nothing more than a revolutionary who casts a jaundiced eye on our monarchs, whether that's the Queen of England or Margaret Atwood, whom CBC Books recently heralded as 'The Queen of CanLit'.

If I'm going to be made to live with the epithet, I'd like to think that I'm polarizing the way a battery is, energizing the flashlight by which you read in the dark only because it has a negative and a positive side. Collected here, under one cover, are my cathodes and my anodes.

—M. L., Toronto, 2016

EVEN LOSING YOU

My fiancée left me, and I thought about villanelles.

Whether you read poetry or not, you probably know at least one villanelle. Two of the most famous poems of the last 100 years are villanelles: 'Do not go gentle into that good night' by Dylan Thomas and 'One Art' by Elizabeth Bishop. A standard one is composed of five tercets, or three-line stanzas, and a concluding quatrain, or four-line stanza. The first and third lines in the opening stanza both rhyme and become refrains that alternate as the last line of the four successive tercets; through the course of the poem, those two lines acquire something like a character, and they build between them a tremendous, heartbreaking relationship as they move towards the final quatrain, where the distance between them is exploded, and they end together in a final couplet. Regardless of the content, a villanelle is about entropy. The slow disordering of love.

I've always been hesitant to say something like that—to claim that a formal construction has an ontological character. But villanelles strike the way that songs written in a minor key do; the actual lyrics can't fundamentally alter the meaning of the thing. The formal narrative is so intense, and so beautiful, that you can stop listening to the words as semantic signifiers and hear them as pure musical characters marching towards their fate.

The first moment I saw her. The first stanza (six years ago, six stanzas). Everything you need to know about a villanelle you learn in the first stanza. I was in from Kingston visiting my sister in Montreal, where she was starting her second year at McGill; she had just moved into a new house with two friends, one of whom, Lisa, I knew. My sister led me through the long hallway of the house on Durocher to the living room, where music was playing. Lisa sat on the far couch. And on the other side of the room, sitting cross-legged in a chair with a glass of wine in her hand, was their other roommate, Amy. Amy: I shook her small hand, sat six feet from her, stared and fell in love. The first thing she did was disagree with me. I was talking about the terrible, failed book I was working on at the time, and she said something about the cheap easiness of its meta-conceit, which insulated it from both failure and success. She was right, of course. We were arguing but it was easy: 'The art of losing isn't hard to master:/so many things seem filled with the intent/to be lost that their loss is no disaster.'

We know the end of things by how they start. What I love about this Elizabeth Bishop villanelle, and those first lines especially, is that the poem is about the villanelle form, and how perfect it is at re-creating the slow disordering of the things we love. All you need to know is the beginning and the rules. Edwin Hubble realized this when he discovered the red shift; looking back in time, to the oldest parts of the universe, he figured out that the rate of expansion of the universe is increasing. One day the galaxies will be speeding away so quickly from each other that their light will no longer reach us. So much darkness is coming—an infinite entropy—that it will be impossible to rediscover that the Big Bang had happened at all.

The middle. This is where the villanelle looks most like love. For the next four stanzas, the poem moderates an exquisite dance between the first and third lines of that first stanza, our main characters. I moved to Montreal for Amy. I wrote *Bloom* and she wrote her LSATs. Some years were mine and some years were hers. We moved to Toronto together, where I published my first book and she started law school. The villanelle, like love, is also the evolution of an argument, with advances and retreats, outbursts and apologies. And wild gambits. After some rocky months in our new apartment, one October morning in our bed, she asked me to marry her. She shook so hard she could hardly hand me the plain gold band. And there between us during those years was my sister Elizabeth, Amy's best friend and mine, the second rhyme around which the tercets revolved.

The final quatrain. Seamus Heaney once said that if we lean upon its etymology, 'conscience' can mean knowing the same thing together. Here the villanelle compels direct address. Dylan Thomas starts his final quatrain with 'And you, my father, there on the sad height.' Bishop begins hers with '—Even losing you (the joking voice, a gesture/I love).' You. You who scrunches her nose and squints when she laughs. The final two lines of a villanelle are one of the great paradoxes in poetry: how is it that a couplet, the coming together of two lines that were built to be united, rings so incredibly sad? The night after she decided it was over, we had a friend to our house for dinner. Amy sat cross-legged in a chair made out of liquor casks we'd bought together. I sat on our couch about six feet away from her. She held a glass of wine in her hand. This is the rhyme. And whereas she'd goaded and prodded and disagreed with me that first night, now she did the scariest thing she could have done. She agreed with me, with everything I said:

> the art of losing's not too hard to master
> though it may look like (*Write* it!) like disaster

PUBLISH LESS

When I was twenty-two, a small literary journal—the name of which, *The Wawa International Fortnightly*, has been changed to protect all involved parties—accepted a poem of mine for publication, my first. I had crossed a threshold that was all but impermeable to lesser mortals, and a new atmosphere now anointed me: I would henceforth and forever be a 'published writer'. And I made damn sure that everyone around me knew it, the scare quotes all but audible. I threw two parties in two cities in my honour, to both of which I brought two bottles of real French Champagne—one to split between those lucky enough to be invited, and one for the 'published writer'. I ordered stacks of the issue, broke the spines at my poem, and placed them conspicuously around my and other people's homes, to be serendipitously stumbled and remarked upon, if not necessarily read. It was the worst work I'd ever publish, a long, imprecise, inelegant howl. But I would never again be so happy to see anything of mine in print.

Nearly ten years later, before a reading at Trent University, I had the opportunity to offer advice to a group of young writers who were about the same age as I was when *The Wawa International Fortnightly* christened me. My advice was: Don't publish. Wait. Read more. Write more. Get better, good enough to be actually, you know, read. Learn to respect the silence you want so badly to break. Once you don't burn for it, you're ready. As the room deoxygenated, I knew that I had breached our unspoken contract. I was there to do the very opposite, to encourage them, to explain the mechanics of the crossing, to enumerate the benefits of being in the priestly published caste, and if not ferry them myself across the rarefied demarcation, then at least direct them to the boatman.

And who could blame them? I too had been one of those unfortunates who wouldn't let the difficult business of producing good writing get in the way of being a writer. Why should I? Writing is hard! And 'good writing' is such, like, a bourgeois idea. Plus everyone knows that contemporary poetry is nothing if not medicine. It's good for me, for you, for all of us really, and better in large doses. It's not supposed to taste good. That's how you know it's working. Don't let your taste buds fool you.

So sitting at my desk at twenty-two, with more ambition than sense (never mind taste), I reverse engineered the problem. I wanted to publish a book. To publish a book I needed to write a book, which took time—time that a grant could buy. According to the Canada Council, to be eligible for a grant I needed to publish at least nine other poems, and had to write at least forty-eight pages of the stuff in order for it to be considered a book (according to the Canada Council, Dante, with only two books of poems under his belt, is not yet an 'established writer'). I swung out on the grants, but within a year I had nonetheless produced a manuscript that I then mailed to the newest, smallest publisher of poetry in Canada, which was a few published titles away from the generous government subsidies that come with publishing poetry. We were each other's easy mark. They offered to publish the book immediately. Even though the work was crap, a compromise both for the author and the publisher, the arrangement, according to the logic of cultural production in this country, was mutually beneficial.

An older writer who I admire intervened, and saved me from Canada's Literary Industrial Complex. Its operating principle is as well intentioned as it is wrong-headed: That the health of a country's literature is best measured using a scale.

Every year, Scott Griffin announces how many hundreds of books the judges of the Griffin Prize had to read— 376!, 491!—as if that were an indication of anything other than the frivolousness with which we publish poetry, and the mirthless duty of its most comprehensive readers (god bless them). But like the munitions factory whose only enemy is an armistice, the Literary Industrial Complex in this country requires a bottomless draught of verbiage, regardless of the quality, for its continued solvency. It dovetails nicely with the post-humanist aesthetic that presently predominates English-language verse, which values the elliptical, the runic, the evasively verbose, in which questions of aesthetic merit dissolve in a sociological and stylistic bath, poems that buy into what Ange Mlinko has called the new generational test of authenticity: 'to write poems that evade all criteria for a "good poem".' And the more of it the better.

All of which is to say that the interconnected system of publishers, granting bodies, magazines, reading series, etc. that, with the purest of intentions, administers and disseminates what we call our literary culture, which by the numbers is as robust as it's ever been, actively encourages, for its own survival, a writer's worst attributes: vanity, assuredness, sophistry, mutual flattery, imprecision, inefficiency and an unselfconscious fluency that is the surest sign of a minor writer. The qualities that contribute to producing great work—skepticism, deliberation, patience—are not in the system's interest. But this is Canada. Here individual achievement doesn't matter as much as our ambient collective hum. We're a country of collectivists, so it's of a piece. To America's Thomas Edison, whose light bulb couldn't be more Promethean and singular, we politely answer with Alexander Graham Bell, whose invention is useless if you don't have a friend.

THE IMITATION GAME

Sometime after Virgil aped Homer but before Kenneth Gold-smith nicked *The New York Times*, poets began robbing one another. It's no surprise: both strands of the Western tradition's double helix—the Hellenic and the Hebraic—begin with thefts, the Greeks absconding with Helen, and Eve filching the fruit. According to Harold Bloom, even *Genesis* isn't sui-generis, having pilfered all its best bits from an earlier ur-text called *The Book of J*. As Beckett—or was it Andy Warhol—first said: 'There's nothing new under the sun.'

When the second poet stole from the very first, he was a larcenist; when the third robbed the first two, he was a traditionalist. Ever since, the relationship between a poet and her predecessors has been described as influence—a fraught intellectual and stylistic exchange by which the old gives birth to the new. Influence's most salient feature, as T.S. Eliot pointed out in 'Tradition and the Individual Talent', is that it is anything but accidental. A literary inheritance may be many things, but it isn't heritable. Safes don't crack and divest themselves; it takes talent, discipline and hard work to steal what someone else earned fair and square.

The critic who has written most obsessively about how and why poets influence one another is Harold Bloom. In *The Anxiety of Influence*, and its follow-up, *A Map of Misreading*, Bloom proposes a kind of Freudian theory of influence whereby poets enter into an *agon*, or struggle, with their forebears. There comes a moment that he calls the 'dialectic of influence', when the young poet realizes that poetry is both outside of her—in the library, in the canon—and nascent inside of her. If she's a 'strong poet', she'll also realize that nearly all she wants to say has been said already, and well. But her ambition is what makes her strong, and so she will 'misread' her most august predecessors, detecting an omission that only she is equipped to redress: herself.

In Bloom's theory of influence, the young poet reads the greats with a simultaneous affinity and anxiety. The line that sings also stings, an agonizing reminder of the newcomer's belatedness. Nevertheless, great poets breed great poets, and you can trace our English lineage like a line of bad blood. Milton comes from Virgil and Spenser, but especially Shakespeare; Keats from Shakespeare and Milton; Tennyson from Keats, etc. In *A Map of Misreading* Bloom charts the *agon* of inheritance as far as A. R. Ammons and John Ashbery, in whose prolix digressiveness Bloom detects an almost crippling belatedness commensurate with our own late hour. By focusing on major careers, he takes for granted that poetry's trajectory is charted by great poets. But in the explosive proliferation of MFA programs since *A Map of Misreading* was published forty years ago, programs that graduate tens of thousands of writers every year, is that still how influence works? Who do poets want to write like today, and why?

———————

I live off a street called Dufferin, a street that is routinely voted the ugliest in Canada, so ugly that a smart phone, in its infinite wisdom, autocorrects its name to 'suffering'. It's ugly because it's democratic. You want to enclose your balcony in opaque, corrugated plastic siding? Go for it. Tired of your Victorian's original brick? Why not redo the exterior in beige bathroom floor tiles. Questions of taste—if they're raised at all—dissolve in a bath of DIY practicality, which prizes speed and thrift. No street in the world looks more like contemporary poetry.

Poetry today is a towering Babel of genres, most as remote from the tradition Bloom charts as Hayden is from Haydn. You can be a sound poet and do nothing but scream. You can be a concrete poet and do nothing but draw. You can be a flarf poet and do nothing but Google. If you're Christian Bök, you write your poems in proteins. If you're Carina Finn, you write your poems in emojis. Even if you're the sort of poet who writes his poems as poems, chances are your primary influences came after Matthew Arnold. For all but the most traditional, in the rush to be contemporary the vast majority of poets have limited their influences to their peers and contiguous predecessors. The anxiety isn't to be great but to be current, and part of a clan. The worst thing a poet can be is traditional; as Eliot wrote a hundred years ago, 'seldom, perhaps, does the word appear except in a phrase of censure.'

Something has changed; the action of influence today isn't *agon* but shibboleth. Contemporary poetry is its own chief—almost exclusive—influence. In Bloom's conception of influence, poets spoke to the future by addressing the past; now poets speak to the present by addressing each other. There are exceptions. Geoffrey Hill is still wrestling with Milton; A.E. Stallings is conversing with Larkin and Yeats and the ancient Greeks; Paul Muldoon is channelling Beckett and Byron. But in the ever-widening river of contemporary poetry, their careers are distinguished tributaries, exceptions that prove the new rule of influence. Style today is a secret handshake, a tribal tattoo, a gang sign, a tag.

Part of this has to do with the fact that poetry has fundamentally changed as an art form since Bloom published *A Map of Misreading* in 1975. As poetry's readership over the last half century has shifted from a general readership to almost exclusively other poets—a shift which coincided with the rise of the

MFA—poetry has become more and more an aspirational craft, like cooking or knitting. You only follow it because you want to do it yourself. The contemporary poet is less artist than artisan, and an influence, like a cross-stitch pattern, is only as powerful as it is replicable. Like a How-To YouTube video, a poet today is only as influential as her style is franchisable for the other poets who constitute her readership.

I think this explains why John Ashbery is the most influential poet writing in English today. As with Freud or Foucault, the problem isn't him but his followers. Ashbery is beloved, endlessly imitated and co-opted because he's easily aped. His slippery, opaque, channel-surfing style dovetails with our postmodern suspicion of meaning, cohesion and form. But more importantly his fun-house logic, associative leaps and sesquipedalian non sequiturs ennoble the initiate's logorrhea, fluency, and mental fog. He helps us evade the problem of having nothing to say that hasn't already been said by not saying very much at all. My country's favourite poet, Al Purdy, is beloved for the same reason: he's the easiest poet to imitate. Contemporary reputations, therefore, are made solely by the self-serving tautology that the more a poet can do for our own practice, the better he must be. We think that a poet like Ashbery or Purdy gives us permission to sound like ourselves, but everyone ends up sounding like everyone else. It's the McDonaldsization of poetry—cheap, quick and everywhere.

As it turns out, Eliot warned us about this very phenomenon in 'Tradition and the Individual Talent'. Like all great poets, he anticipated us before we were even ourselves. He wrote: 'If the only form of tradition, of handing down, consisted in following the ways of the immediate generation before us in a blind or timid adherence to its successes, "tradition" should be positively discouraged.' It's a biting irony that the revolution he helped usher in would devolve into the very orthodoxy he warned us against. So much poetry since Eliot has fetishized our belatedness, and prioritized it as being different from what came before, not only in degree, but also in kind. Read his warning one more time; like a good traditionalist, he was writing in the past tense but talking about the future.

LEONARD COHEN

I paid twenty bucks to see *Watchmen* in the theatre on its opening weekend. It was a dark time. At one point, two comically hot, be-rubbered superheroes start fucking in a hovercraft made to look like an owl, accompanied by the cruise-ship-lounge schmaltz of Leonard Cohen's 'Hallelujah'. A close-up of some late-game pelvic thrusting cuts to an exterior shot of the hover-owl spewing a column of fire into the buxom, unblemished clouds as Leonard and the ladies belt out the chorus. The synthesizer wails. 'Hallelujah': This, I thought, is the apotheosis of the thing. Even Jeff Buckley's reanimated holo-corpse doing his unimpeachable version at Coachella wouldn't hold a candle to this. The guy next to me, sufficiently trained in the Simon Cowell school of criticism, turned to his girlfriend and said: 'Whoever's covering this is just butchering it.'

To appreciate what makes Leonard Cohen great—and also what makes him not-so-great—you first need to concede that he was, as Auden said of Yeats, 'silly like us'. Sylvie Simmons's incisive new biography, *I'm Your Man*, is an essential tool in the enterprise, steering clear, for the most part, of the Oprah-lens hagiography that has dominated the discourse about Cohen for the last fifty years.

To be fair, Cohen's cultivated persona is itself a deliberate work of art forged by a deft artificer. By his early teens, he'd sharpened his talent for hypnotism—with the aid of a pencil—to the point where he could get the maid to undress in his privileged family's drawing room. Decades later, stoned out of his skull on Mandrax, he could pacify a crowd of half a million riotously fucked hippies at the Isle of Wight Festival with his mannered saintliness. Erica Pomerance, a McGill undergraduate with whom he was having an affair while living with Marianne of 'So-Long' fame, describes his famous professional cool: 'He didn't run after journalists, getting himself publicized; his magnetism is such that it's like a boat creating a wake and people are drawn to him and his ideas.'

But the private Cohen wasn't quite so laissez-faire with, to borrow a mixed metaphor, the magnetism of his wake; such studied self-deprecation glossed a self-conscious megalomania. He wasn't averse to writing his own celebratory copy (in the third person) for the back covers of his early books of poetry. He hailed *Flowers for Hitler*, in a letter to his publisher Jack McClelland, 'a masterpiece' (it isn't). He characterized *Beautiful Losers*—his derivatively Joycean novel that hasn't aged very well—as a 'religious epic of incomparable beauty'.

In other words, the discrepancy between the public and private Cohen reveals not the consistency of a saint, but the inconstancy of a sinner. And more than that, the man who was self-avowedly 'born in a suit', and was renowned for his charm, had a habit of exhibiting wickedly bad taste. In 1963, at a symposium on the future of Canadian Judaism, Cohen harangued the Montreal Jewish community—many of whom were members of what Cohen described as the 'Dachau Generation'—for having eschewed the spiritual for the material. And yet some three years later, he'd transition into a career in music primarily because 'it was an economic solution to the problem of making a living and being a writer.' He warned friends of the perils of false messiahs and yet submitted to just about every religion and charlatan on offer, including Scientology and the 'catastrophist' Immanuel Velikovsky, who believed that human anxiety was caused by comets colliding (religion is exactly what we should expect to find flowering in the heart of someone taking literature too seriously).

Even his taste in muses could be weird. It turns out that Cohen's appraisal of Suzanne (Verdal) as 'half-crazy' was probably too generous by half. When Leonard would visit her apartment for those famous tea and oranges, she would observe a solemn ritual: 'I would light a candle to invoke the Spirit of Poetry—I called the flame Anastasia, don't ask me why.' She called the flame Anastasia. And for all the cultured disgust for war in his songs and poems, he twice volunteered for it—first during the Cuban revolution, but that was more about getting away from Marianne; and second during the Yom Kippur War, but that was more about getting away from Suzanne (Elrod) and his young son Adam. He told *ZigZag* magazine in 1974: 'War is wonderful. They'll never stamp it out. It's one of the times people can act their best.' He never saw action.

Ickiest of all is how Cohen the Ladies' (and Lady's) Man treated his ladies, whom he so publicly celebrated. The high-minded free love of the 1960s didn't age well as Cohen dragged it through the decades. He pleaded in letters for Suzanne to move to Montreal with her son, and a couple of months after she did, Cohen split for Cuba (he returned home at the behest of his mother). When his son Adam was born in Montreal, Cohen split for the Chelsea Hotel. The CBC reporter Malka Marom recalls an interview she did with Cohen in his garden-shed writing room in 1974, with his family at home: 'Soon after I set up the recording equipment, Leonard's hand went right underneath my skirt. I said, "What are you doing?" and he said, "This is the real dialogue," or something to that effect.'

The word that comes to mind here is 'tacky'. And the tackiness that made Cohen distasteful as a man is exactly what makes him fascinating in his most enduring work, *Various Positions* and *The Future*. His lyricism in those two albums is at its most formally accomplished, but undercutting its majesty is the

Closing-Set-at-the-Lido-Bar-in-Hell schmaltz of his beloved Casio synthesizer. His early guitar albums do nothing for me; as for his poetry, his first book is wonderful, but after that it's a game of diminishing returns. But I think what makes those two albums great is that Cohen was willing to undermine the most spectacular poetry he'd ever written with deliberately tacky orchestration. He'd finally found a musical form that embodied a lyric he'd been working on for years (and an ethos he'd been perfecting for a half-century): 'Forget your perfect offering./There is a crack in everything./That's how the light gets in.'

'Hallelujah' has been covered some 300 times. I don't think that would be the case if Cohen hadn't encased it in the ludicrous musical carapace of his Casio. It's as if the form of the song is courting a kind of perfection that he himself wouldn't dare attempt—the crack through which the light gets in. So there's something almost holy in the image of Alexandra Burke singing the living Christ out of the song in front of Simon Cowell—the closest thing we have to a St. Peter—who nods for all of us and grants Cohen a kind of proxy absolution.

JOHN THOMPSON

Before Twitter, the best way for a poet to advance his career was by killing himself. The sort of splashy gesture that might catch the distractible eye of a reporter, it also has the happy side effect of radically reducing a poet's cost of living. The only obvious drawback is that he has to resign himself to being misunderstood.

End it all and everything you've ever written is transposed into the score of your demise. In an instant, your oeuvre becomes a long, rather mannered suicide note. Your corpus becomes your corpse, and readers will dissect it like pathologists. Behind every darkly turned phrase they'll detect the angel of death. Reading the poem 'Edge', from the end of Sylvia Plath's *Ariel*, everybody knows—wrongly—she could only have been thinking of one thing when she wrote: 'The woman is perfected./Her dead/Body wears the smile of accomplishment.' In other words, killing yourself encourages people to read poetry in the worst possible way, as an enigma—what is the poet *trying to say?*—waiting to be deciphered.

About this at least, Margaret Atwood was right: Canadian poets have for the most part been survivors when it comes to suicide. Having killed ourselves in fewer numbers, we've also produced fewer books that can be interpreted as suicide notes like Berryman's *Dream Songs*. Richard Outram's death by his own hand seems to have had more to do with the despair of losing his companion, collaborator and wife at the end of a long life than with his succumbing to a lifelong depression; his suicide doesn't transform his body of work either. Our only notable exception is the great John Thompson, whose mysterious death at thirty-eight, of either suicide or accidental overdose, casts a pall over his mercurial masterpiece, *Stilt Jack*.

Born in England during the Second World War, John Thompson arrived in Canada in the autumn of 1966, having accepted an appointment as assistant professor of English at Mount Allison University in Sackville, New Brunswick. An avid outdoorsman and fisherman, he moved his family—his wife, Meredith, and their two-year-old daughter—to an idyllic little farmhouse where he wrote the mostly happy poems of his first collection, the promising but innocuous *At the Edge of the Chopping There Are No Secrets*.

Thompson, though, liked to drink. Peter Sanger's generous and comprehensive introduction to Thompson's *Collected Poems* recounts how towards the end of the '60s, Thompson's drinking, and what Sanger calls his 'uncompromising presence (or absence)' began to complicate his life. In a story as old as CanLit itself, a small, prurient group of English professors felt that Thompson was 'irresponsible', 'a subversive and a failure as a writer', and pressured the university to withhold tenure from him when his four-year probationary term of employment expired. Although there was a larger group of professors—and indeed, students—who disagreed with the mischaracterization, in the spring of 1970 the university president, one L.H. Cragg, wrote a letter to the future author of *Stilt Jack* explaining how 'most of the tenured members of your Department entertain serious doubts about your potential.' For many of Thompson's admirers, the episode is a testament to the radical incompetence of the Mount Allison English department, its abject failure in firing a writer who in short order would matriculate from its faculty to its syllabus.

The students of Mount Allison ended up revolting, and eventually the university reinstated Thompson. But by 1973, the year Anansi published his first book, Thompson's life was disintegrating. His wife and daughter left him, and the house he'd moved into was isolated, freezing and dilapidated. By Sanger's account, Thompson's drinking was now more or less out of control. It was under these conditions he began to compose *Stilt Jack*.

Published posthumously, *Stilt Jack* is a collection of thirty-eight ghazals, a poem for every year of Thompson's life. He includes a brief primer on the form as an introduction, where he explains the ghazal's origin in ninth-century Persia, and its formal conventions. The ghazal, he writes, 'proceeds by couplets which (and here, perhaps, is the great interest in the form for Western writers) have no necessary logical, progressive, narrative, thematic (or whatever) connection.'

That's not quite right though, as the poems in *Stilt Jack* do have a kind of logic—alcoholic logic. Thompson ends his introduction by writing: 'The ghazal has been called "drunken and amatory" and I think it is.' Thompson's interest in drinking, in other words, wasn't strictly recreational. In 1962 he published a translation of Rimbaud's 'The Drunken Boat'. In 1966, he edited and helped translate a book on Paul Claudel and his *'l'ivresse poetique'*, which Thompson himself rendered as 'poetic drunkenness'. And in *Stilt Jack*, he managed, more than any poet since Baudelaire, to distill the feeling—and the meaning—of being intoxicated.

The first poem opens with a tone any barfly will recognize, the self-admonishing second person of your conscience telling you that you're ruined: 'Now you have burned your books: you'll go/with nothing but your blind, stupefied heart.' But the formal conventions of the ghazal don't let Thompson dwell in melancholy very long, and soon his spirit is buoyant again with the impossible optimism of a boozehound trying out the old geographical solution: 'In this place we might be happy; blue-/winged teal, blacks, bats, steam/ from cows dreaming in frost.' His state of mind turns not only between poems, but between lines, which can start despairingly and end carefree: 'I can't talk to God. Tonight, I dug/three hills of potatoes. Sadness, what's that?' Or even faster, when he pivots on the most devastating comma in Canadian poetry: 'Breaking my heart, laughing.' He turns from prophet to couch potato in a colon: 'Sometimes I think the stars scrape at my door, wanting in:/I'm watching the hockey game.' You get the sense that Thompson's punctuation is well irrigated.

In other words, *Stilt Jack* transforms the formal conventions of the ghazal—its elisions, its violent mood shifts and pirouettes of sense—into the sound of a mind in its cups. I mean that as a compliment. It's easy in our cultural milieu to conclude that a poet with Thompson's thirst was indulging his self-destruction, aestheticizing it, but Thompson's poetic inebriation isn't the slacker, secular blotto of a Charles Bukowski or an Al Purdy, but rather the resigned, world-weary, almost religious drunkenness of Baudelaire, who, tongue firmly in cheek, advised: 'Always be drunk. That's all there is to it … on wine, poetry, or on virtue, as you wish.'

Sanger, in his introduction, notes that Thompson would, in conversation, call his poems 'guzzles', which, he'd explain, was the truer pronunciation. 'The pun, I suspect,' Sanger dryly notes, 'had more sinister implications than some of his friends realized.' Sinister maybe, but telling too, as Thompson was making the same connection as Baudelaire between the shit-faced state and the poetic sensibility. Much ink has been spilled about the 'elemental' nature of Thompson's work, and it's true—his poems are full of irreducible bases to which his mind frequently returns: fire, books, blood, hooks, fish, stones, birds, houses, wives. As anyone who drinks—especially anyone who drinks alone—knows, that's what booze does, boiling off the superfluity and imperfections of a day until all that's left is the insoluble. It's the distillation that complicates your life as it clarifies your mind.

The reason why booze is such a potent wellspring for Thompson is because it gives him access to the contradictions that reside at the heart of all great poetry. Booze is the poison that fortifies, the chaos that clarifies, the love that banishes. Liquor's logic is the logic of the dialectic, thesis and antithesis bound terribly and inextricably together. Its twin impulses are Freud's Eros and Thanatos, driving us to ecstasy as we approach extinction. It's booze that wrote: 'in the middle of life, we are in death.' It's booze that asks Hamlet's famous question, which isn't just the question of poetry, but the question of living: why love the thing that will eventually break our heart and then destroy us, life itself? It's the logic of alcohol that gives *Stilt Jack* its power, its convivial elisions and boozy about-faces, to vacillate between joy and desolation, humour and horror, life and death.

Thompson wrote in his introduction that there is no narrative to the ghazal, but there is one in *Stilt Jack*. It's the story of travelling the harrowing passage of all great poetry, what Eliot described as 'the gradual extinction of personality'. Often overlooked about Thompson, overshadowed by the tragic circumstances of his death, is how funny he was. David McGimpsey could have written this, but John Thompson did: 'Yeats. Yeats. Yeats. Yeats. Yeats. Yeats. Yeats./Why wouldn't the man shut up?' Michael Robbins could have written this: 'I'll read Keats and eye the weather too,/smoke cigarettes, watch Captain Kangaroo.' But as the book progresses, you get a sense that the wheels are falling off. This is especially true of how Thompson writes about liquor. It starts off charming and funny: 'I have so many beer bottles, I'll be rich.' A foreboding chill creeps in mid-collection: 'How far down on whiskey row am I?' By the end, it's terrifying: 'Love, look at my wounds, the shame I've drunk—/I wouldn't wish such suffering on my bitterest enemy.' Of course, we should give Thompson enough credit to consider that the lyric 'I' could be a literary construction distinct from Thompson himself, and that its dissolution might be for aesthetic effect. But here's the part everyone always forgets from that Eliot quotation: 'only those who have personality and emotions know what it means to want to escape from those things.'

What's also important to remember about *Stilt Jack*—something too often forgotten when a poet kills himself—is how radically alive the book is, and how hard it fights against despair. Some of Thompson's more aphoristic couplets feel cribbed from the gospels: 'Celebrate. Celebrate. Celebrate./Death cannot celebrate thee.' or 'If there's joy for one day, there is, there is:/they that sow in tears: shall reap in joy.' My favourite is this, with its desolation-row logic that shines so darkly: 'If I give everything away/it's because I want to take everything.'

Thompson didn't so much give everything away than he had everything taken from him. A failed romance and a sabbatical year in Toronto were punctuated in September of 1974, when his house in New Brunswick—and the books in it—burned down. It was as if the prophetic lines from the first and last poems of *Stilt Jack* were coming true. His divorce was finalized in 1975 and he went to live alone in a small apartment in Sackville. He wrote his will, in which he specified his desire to be buried in a pine box, just like in *Stilt Jack*. There's a curiously formal technique that Thompson uses throughout *Stilt*

Jack that's worth mentioning here. In both individual poems, and throughout the book as a whole, Thompson returns to ideas and phrases and images that he's introduced earlier, like a prognostication that's become fact, a kind of call and response. By 1975, it looked like Thompson's life was echoing his book. Except for one prophecy, which hadn't jumped his poems to his life: suicide. In *Stilt Jack* the speaker twice turns his thoughts darkly to a shotgun. First, he writes: 'Pigs fattened on boiled potatoes; horses mooning in hay:/in the woodshed he blew his head off with a shotgun.' Thompson did in fact own a shotgun, which he called Tobin. In Ghazal XVI he writes: 'I'll suck oil from Tobin's steel and walnut.'

Then, in one of the final ironies of his brief life, in the spring of 1975, Thompson, drunk one night, fired a gun into the air from his backyard. A neighbour phoned the police who came and confiscated Tobin and another rifle. He was barred, by court order, from possessing a weapon for five years. It was Thompson's final insult. He delivered the manuscript of *Stilt Jack* and phoned his editor—and erstwhile lover—to whom he confessed that he couldn't quit drinking, because he couldn't live without 'joy and celebration in my life'. Later that night, he aspirated on his own vomit. Liquor and psychiatric medication were found in his blood, but whether he intended to kill himself couldn't be determined. Unlike the definitive suicides of Plath or Berryman, even Thompson's death is Thompsonian, his thirty-eighth year reverberating with the hopeful ambiguity of his thirty-eighth ghazal: 'Will it all come back to me?/Or just leave.'

Be it resolved that the following are off-limits to Canadian poets indefinitely: Tom Thomson, Glenn Gould (and his Chickering piano), fishing (especially as a metaphor), the Northwest Passage, the Franklin Expedition and birdsong. Step away from the wood stove: give us instead the poem Christian Bök has challenged us to write, whose action revolves around the word 'microwaveable'. Dear Don McKay, I want to read 'The Song for the Song of the SR-71 Blackbird'. Find and replace: 'Henry Hudson' with 'Felix Baumgartner'.

And yet—and yet. Life, too, is a cliché, with its extenuating franchise of birth, love and death, its rote performances of joy and grief. The contemporary poet navigating her way to a new style hazards the ice-jams of two opposing poles: the well-worn and unadorned plain style of Edward Arlington Robinson and Edward Thomas and Robert Frost, or the more treacherous, fashionable narrows of lexical and syntactic idiosyncrasy. While I applaud the discoveries of the latter, I think more and more that landfall by way of the former is the more impressive feat.

Part of that is because, as well-travelled as it is and by such titanic talents, new discoveries in the plain style are less likely, and less frequent. And that's why James Pollock's debut, *Sailing to Babylon* (which had hardly left port before it was nominated for this year's [2012] Governor General's Award), is such a noteworthy book. Of the topics I advise to steer clear of, he writes about: Glenn Gould (and his Chickering piano), the Northwest Passage (twice), the Franklin Expedition and birdsong.

But in Pollock's unadorned style, forged as it is in traditional forms—blank verse, rhyming couplets, sonnets, terza rima—we get a vision of an old world, freighted with history, and still able to astonish itself with the novelty of its recurrence.

To Pollock, discovery is the rediscovery of language itself. Take the opening poem, 'Northwest Passage', where the grammar of the poem is the story. The action of the ice freezing around Franklin's doomed expedition is enacted by the subordinate clauses and phrases that pile up like 'steeples / of jagged ice' and prevent a full single sentence from reaching its fatal end, until the poem's end.

'See how foolish you have been,' Pollock concludes, 'forcing your way by will across a land / that can't be forced, but must be understood, / toward a passage just now breaking up within.' Language is landscape, and its cartography is poetry's only navigable fact.

If 'Northwest Passage' succeeds precisely because it passes Ezra Pound's test that a poem's technique, appropriately warped by its subject, reveals the sincerity of a poet, a poem such as 'Glenn Gould on the Telephone' fails for the very same reason. The poem finds Gould on tour in Tel Aviv in 1958, recounting his performance there of Beethoven (who he was terrible at interpreting), when suddenly Gould could 'hear the concerto with my inward ear, / which is to say I heard my inner self.' But that musical revelation of Gould's transcendence is encased in the rather workmanlike verse paragraphs of an unrhymed dramatic monologue. A form with higher musical stakes would have been far more convincing.

But Pollock is playing a high-stakes game, not only in his deployment of lexically unadorned poems cast in traditional forms, but also in the fact that he deploys so few of them: *Sailing to Babylon* contains eighteen poems that span some sixty pages. Here we should stand and applaud on principle; this business of 100-page books of poetry is preposterous. No one can produce that much good new poetry every four years. Pollock wagers the success of the book on a single poem, the concluding 'Quarry Park', a twenty-two-page update of Dante in near-flawless terza rima. His remarkable work in that tricky form feels like a direct rebuke of Robert Pinsky's justification for using half- or slant-rhyme in his rendition of Dante, when he proposed that English is a rhyme-poor language. Pollock has an excellent ear for perfect rhyme and only very rarely does it feel as if he's warping the sense of a line for the sake of its sound.

In 'Quarry Park', Pollock is a new Dante, navigating a dark wood in the middle of life, but Virgil, his guide, is recast as Pollock's own young son; throughout the poem the erudite Pollock is always trailing behind his young master, belatedly aestheticizing what his two-and-a-half-year-old son can appreciate viscerally—an abandoned campsite, climbing trees, ants farming and eating aphids, and yes, a cardinal's song. The enduring beauty of 'Quarry Park', and of *Sailing to Babylon* as a whole, is in the way both young seekers find renewal in what preceded them and endures:

> it all fills
>
> me with such longing, for God knows how frail
> our lives and their monuments are, and yet
> how beautiful the ruins that prevail
>
> even in the midst of death; how we forget,
> and how our forgetting makes us homeless,
> until we dig ourselves out of this debt
>
> we owe the giant past for making us
> ourselves.

MATTHEW TIERNEY

In 1802, Samuel Taylor Coleridge started sitting in on the chemistry lectures of one Humphry Davy. His classmates at the Royal Institution of London found this odd. What was a poet doing, one of his classmates asked, dithering with a subject so incongruous with his own? 'I attend Davy's lectures,' Coleridge replied, 'to increase my stock of metaphors.'

Canadian poets have gone back to the academy. In the last fifteen years a whole away-party of poets has materialized on the transporter deck. Their verse has gone Borg, been assimilated, the organic lyric body retrofitted and be-lasered with high-tech implants. Hot courses include chemistry (Christian Bök, Adam Dickinson), aerodynamics (Jake Mooney) and cognitive science (Karen Solie, Linda Besner, Ken Babstock), but the real ticket is physics, and one of the key hybridists in the field is Matthew Tierney, whose author bio used to read: 'In the second year of his undergraduate degree, he switched majors from physics to English.' His new collection, *Probably Inevitable* (Coach House Books), is one of the most exciting books in this particularly Canadian sub-genre.

The poems in *Probably Inevitable* succeed where other science-minded poems fail because despite their erudition and dizzying range of reference, they're still romancing the 'breadth between feeling and knowing'. 'What a moron the heart is,' he writes, a sentiment shared by many of the science poets whose work, for all its conceptual savvy, all too often feels bereft of feeling. But Tierney doesn't really mean it; the line appears in the poem 'Suede Spats', a meandering meditation on the formation of the universe, during a date at a '50s-style milkshake diner. What excites Tierney isn't the cold mechanics that brought the couple to this moment, but the pleasure it engenders, 'a joy not possible/before the big bang made creation some sweet place.'

I don't want to give you the impression that Tierney's light on the science. He isn't. My IP address was working Wikipedia something fierce with his references to the 'Planck time interval', 'Gordian knots' and 'lemniscates'. One of these poems was published in *American Scientist*, for god's sake. But the weakest poems in the book are the ones made of long blocks of free-verse paragraphs that lean most heavily on the Googleable. That stuff is enjoying something of a moment right now; it's *vers libre* GZA for MFAs (though Tierney is far, far better at it than almost anyone). What's really incredible is to see Tierney making it new in the old way, in the most jaw-dropping poem in the book, the long poem 'That Stratospheric Streak My Green Filament', a sort of Cloud Atlas done by Shelley. I have no clue what the title means, but I don't need to when I can read Tierney work images such as: 'Leafless season, the tallest cedars/like stags knocking antlers.' Or: 'Pages turn themselves in the librarian's lap, or/a butterfly on a twig suns its wings.' Or: 'speeding past the old street: gone the creek,/gone the creek's frogs after school.'

Probably Inevitable is skeptical of, among lots of other things, the very idea of time itself, but I think chronology explains why Tierney's poems work when others' fail. The key is in that old bio. Tierney wasn't flashing his chops there; he was telling us his priorities had shifted. Poetry comes first for him now. Most of the new science-informed poets, I think, are going about it in the opposite order, all too willing to sacrifice the poetry if the science calls for it, killing the organic flesh in the name of a Borg graft. If you gathered all the poets of Tierney's ilk together, sat them down in a room—a thousand monkeys working at a thousand typewriters for eternity—and asked them to write about the cosmological phenomena known as the red shift, only Tierney could come up with something so beautiful, so linguistically earned, so sweetly charming and weird as this: '400 billion Andromedas gone like/400 billion Jimmy Hoffas in a trunk.' And that's precisely because Tierney understands, like Coleridge, that science can solve the problems of science, but it can't solve the problems of poetry.

Who is the I who reads poems when I read poems? The mind is not its own place; I is another. But not just another: other anothers too. So argues poet, scholar and critic Maureen N. McLane in her new [2012] collection of criticism, *My Poets*, a book that may do more to change the way we think and write about poems than any since Paul Muldoon's *The End of the Poem*.

My Poets is the autobiography of a divided pronoun. Its cover art is instructive: two half-portraits, of William Carlos Williams and Emily Dickinson (each looking uncannily like the other), fused man-to-woman down the nose to create a new hybrid. McLane's essays think similarly; poets are read through other poets; the prose hotwires different styles and rhetorical strategies; seemingly contradictory aesthetics are hybridized to create new chimeras of sense.

The book itself is divided too, in that it's as much a collection of incisive and angular close readings as it is the spiritual biography of McLane's partitioned self, specifically her love for another woman in the midst of McLane's heterosexual marriage. Chaucer, as the book's first essay so brilliantly notes, would call this a 'Kankedort': 'Isolate, peculiar, rare, obsolete, it surfaces in the language only once ... in Chaucer's *Troilus and Criseyde* ... speculatively defined as a "difficult situation"' and 'further glossed in the OED as "a state of suspense; a critical position; an awkward affair".'

Over the course of *My Poets*, in essays on Elizabeth Bishop, William Carlos Williams, Marianne Moore, H.D., Louise Glück, Fanny Howe, Dickinson and Shelley, McLane proves that the kankedort is also the seat of poetry, and the appreciation thereof. She writes: 'I needed a kind of saving no one would offer and I could not provide myself. I read myself into all the contradictions.' And so in her essay on Bishop, which is written in the style of Gertrude Stein, she writes: 'My Elizabeth Bishop begins with Gertrude Stein. This is not usual.' Bizarre even; but by its second page, it feels, like the best poems, to be equally alien and inevitable. She could be writing about her essay itself when she writes about Stein: 'She is of course ridiculous until she's not and then she both is and is not ridiculous.'

The central division in McLane as critic is the division between thought and feeling, and she charts its long dialogic course. In the essay 'My Impasse', she recounts her first embarrassing stabs at reading poetry in her university classes (she even includes a photocopy of her early reading copy of Frank O'Hara's 'The Day Lady Died', hesitantly annotated with the sort of cringe-worthy marginalia we all have) and writes:

I am fascinated by that threshold where one hovers, not getting it yet wanting to get it. Where a tentative desire contends with frustration. Where frustration may be converted into desire, and desire into some provisional illumination.

This willingness to let the heart lead the head (or sound lead sense) is a temperament that permeates McLane's essays. She writes that 'some of (H.D.'s) poems bypassed my brain and registered directly on the nerve endings' and that Williams's 'best poems are like Keats's ... proved upon the pulse.' But don't be fooled; when McLane gets around to the thinking, it's never just appreciative puffery. Writing about her beloved H.D., McLane declares: 'Out of some 600 pages perhaps some 50 are dear to me.' And later, referencing the world's first anthologist, 1st-century Greek poet Meleager's appraisal of Sappho:

It is no dispraise to be a poet best served by an anthology, a rigorously pruned selected—no dispraise particularly for this poet, who knew very well that 'anthology' comes from the Greek: a gathering of flowers. 'Little, but all roses'.

The achievement of *My Poets* is the convincing case it makes that a reader's real strength is her ability to cultivate an inconsistency of taste, which McLane argues is the inheritance of maturity. The goal is not to circle the square of one's incongruities, but rather, when thinking alone will not bridge the partitioned self, to trust in feeling. Or put another way, it's worth remembering that in Horace's dictum on what poetry must be—*dulce et utile*—pleasurable comes before instructive. About her romantic kankedort she writes: 'I had fallen in love with another but not it would seem out of love with him. This was unwieldly. This was worse: It was a contradiction, a flaw in the world.' She may as well be writing about seemingly contradictory poets; two that come to my mind are Emerson ('There is a crack in everything God has made') and Cohen ('There is a crack in everything. / That's how the light gets in.')

On very few occasions, McLane's essays suffered from what she diagnoses in Bishop, that she might be 'praised for the very thing that is a fault'. The list essays and some of the ventriloquism can feel like a stylistic liability masquerading as an asset. But on the whole these arguments with oneself feel more like poetry than rhetoric, as Yeats would put it; *My Poets* is not just criticism, but art. It's the sort of book you finish and say, 'I wish I'd written that.'

LUCRETIUS

In the winter of 1417, an Italian humanist and former papal secretary named Poggio Bracciolini, on horseback and all alone in Southern Germany, discovered a very old book. He had recently found himself masterless and unemployed after Pope John XXIII, under whom Poggio had served as Apostolic Secretary, a position of enormous power and prestige, had been stripped of his title and imprisoned. And so Poggio found himself free to indulge in his life's true work: hunting for the lost books of antiquity. In the library of a monastery—most likely the remote Benedictine Abbey of Fulda—Poggio, scanning the chief librarian's catalogue, came across an author whose name he would have recognized from the enthusiastic writings of Cicero and Ovid: Titus Lucretius Carus, a Roman poet of the first century BCE.

Poggio and his humanist friends would have known that Cicero once wrote that 'the poetry of Lucretius … is rich in brilliant genius, yet highly artistic', and that Ovid said 'the verses of sublime Lucretius are destined to perish only when a single day will consign the world to destruction.' But perish they did, not in a single day, but over the slow amnesia of centuries, and for 1,000 years, he lived only as a rumour until Poggio unshelved his radically dangerous epic poem '*De rerum natura*' ('On the Nature of Things').

Harvard professor Stephen Greenblatt thrillingly recounts this discovery and the poem's transformative effect on the Western mind in his excellent new book *The Swerve: How the World Became Modern* [2011]. That effect, according to Greenblatt, was nothing short of stirring the Renaissance, prefiguring the Enlightenment and influencing the Declaration of Independence. Of course, he doesn't claim that the poem caused the Renaissance, but rather that the Epicurean injunction that the pursuit of pleasure—or as Jefferson, an avowed Lucretian, famously put it, 'the pursuit of happiness'—and the appreciation of beauty are the most noble purposes of human life, fuelled and inspired the European imagination enough to send it swerving from Medievalism.

Besides being an aesthetically astounding poem—we now know that '*De rerum natura*' was the principal Latin influence on the greatest of Roman poets, Virgil, in emulation in his Georgics and refutation in *The Aeneid*—it's hard to overstate how radically prescient and threatening the philosophy that underlies it is. Greenblatt does a marvellous job of showing how, through the millennia, admirers of Lucretius, from Cicero to Poggio to his first English translator, Lucy Hutchinson, went to great lengths to gloss their enthusiasm for the poem as an aesthetic object with an incredulity towards its philosophical message. Even today, readers of this column may well find what Lucretius thinks 'offensive'. He's the only ancient poet whose ideas are still radical.

So, what did Lucretius believe? He was, to put it simply, the world's first materialist. He was a deist; he thought that if the gods did exist, they couldn't possibly, by virtue of their divinity, be interested in the lives of human beings, and so were indifferent to our propitiations and misdeeds. He believed that religion, the institutionalization of superstition, was the chief cause of human mischief and unhappiness. He proposed that all matter, from humans to oceans to planets, is composed of tiny, indivisible, eternal particles that are in constant motion in an infinite void, and that nothing outside of matter exists. He thought the universe had no creator, and that divine providence is a dangerous fantasy. He said that change comes into the world when atoms 'swerve' (*climamen* in the Latin) into one another, setting off a ceaseless chain of collisions, and that the swerve— and not a God—is the source of free will. He believed that all living beings evolved through a long process of natural trial and error, and that the successfulness of adaptations is the function that determined an animal's survival. He said there were no interruptions in the natural order, no miracles. He believed that humans arose out of a larger material process by which we are connected to all things, living and inert. He thought the universe is intelligible, and that systematized inquiry into the material world makes us more free. And finally, he thought that the soul dies when the body dies, and that there is no afterlife, and because of that there's no reason to fear death (since you won't be around to fear it). Since this is the only life we have, our noblest goal is the pursuit of pleasure and beauty and the avoidance of pain.

So yes, the gentleman was ahead of his time. Perhaps most radically, Lucretius said that religion reaches its apotheosis in a single image: that of a father killing his child to achieve a supernatural end. Remember that Lucretius died before Jesus of Nazareth was born, never mind crucified; he may have been acquainted with the Jewish holy books, and the story of Isaac, but he never refers to them. And Islam was still hundreds of years away (though we refer to the three great monotheisms as Abrahamic). Instead, he bewails the terrifying superstition that led Iphigenia, daughter of Agamemnon,

'To be impurely slaughtered, at the age when she should have wed. Sorrowful sacrifice slain at her father's hand instead. All this for fair and favourable winds to sail the fleet along!—So potent was Religion in persuading to do wrong.'

Greenblatt's case for Lucretius being central to the Renaissance can at times feel thin, but he leaves little doubt that we're modern insofar as we're Lucretian. Not because we now believe what Lucretius believed about atomic theory or evolution or materialism or free will; in many ways, the fact that those turned out to be true were Lucretian swerves themselves (though the scientific method by which we came to discover them is Lucretian, too).

The process of modernization is one of uncentring Man; Copernicus, Galileo, Giordano Bruno, Shakespeare, Newton, Darwin, Albert Einstein, Thomas Jefferson, Karl Marx, Frederick Douglass and Susan B. Anthony (in whose case it was about uncentring man, not Man) all made us modern in so far as they convinced us that no human, like no place in Lucretian physics, is the centre of things. And perhaps the most threatening Lucretian idea of all is that by disabusing ourselves of our misapprehensions, our superstitions and intellectual neurosis, we are made more free; understanding things as they are generates a deep and abiding wonder. Though I must say the improbable story of Poggio rediscovering Lucretius—the demolition man of divine providence—is enough to strain the skepticism of even the most devout materialist.

TIM LILBURN

Like a prescription drug commercial, Tim Lilburn's *Assiniboia* gloats about its triumph in treating the disease we assume we have. The back cover gasconades that Lilburn 'resituate[s] the root of human singing deep in the body's core', which 'amounts to a resuscitation of singing itself.' Though William Barnes, Gerard Manley Hopkins and Ted Hughes all made similar boasts for themselves, this new and improved gut-singing will reimburse nothing less than 'the theft that founds our nation', Lilburn's appraisal of the sale of Rupert's Land and the North West Territory. By resurrecting Louis Riel and members of his provisional government, *Assiniboia* is 'bent on overturning more than a century of colonial practice.' This is behind-the-counter medicine that deserves to be strictly controlled.

Lilburn's own unselfconscious introduction tells us that his book attempts to summon *Assiniboia*'s 'imaginal state, polyglot ... local, mixed race, Catholic-mystical' before it was 'destroyed by armies from central Canada'. The book takes the form of two 'choral performances' (really just two short suites of poems) sandwiching a masque, 'a polis, (a) repeopling of western Canada' which includes Sara Riel, Louis's sister, the Catholic mystic who was convinced that her recovery from pneumonia was divinely ordained, Calypso, Odysseus, Suhrawardi, the Persian mystic, and of course, Dionysus. But because in Lilburn's mind *Assiniboia* is an 'unlimited democracy ... where everything has franchise', it also includes 'the dead, animals, plants, wished-for presences' and an anthropomorphized landform that Lilburn calls 'Cabri man'. All of these bits are marshalled like antibiotics against the 'many ... old imperial gestures (that) remain still vigorous among us.' To avoid any confusion, the pharmacist has appended the following note: 'let this recital be applied to the wound.'

Once we start taking Lilburn as directed, though, we become acquainted with the deleterious side effects: dry mouth, bloating, the runs. For decades, Lilburn, a trained Jesuit, has been preaching his Gospel of Strangeness. In his book of essays *Living in the World As If It Were Home*, he famously wrote: 'the world seen deeply eludes all names; it is not like anything else, it is not the sign of something else. It is itself. It is a towering strangeness.' One must appreciate how strange it is for a poet to say that the world is not 'the sign of something else' because that is what poetry *is*: anthropomorphizing nature by transubstantiating it into the most human elements—language and metaphor. Lilburn's hectoring Pentecostal maximalism demands that the true world, the world represented by Catholic mysticism, Dionysus and Riel, is truest when it's most unlike itself, and so we get very little of Riel, of Sara, of Calypso, of the human reality of the time—of any humans really. Instead we get lots and lots of this, from a poem called 'Exegesis':

'The milkweed hold still, holds still
for the eschatologically optimistic hermeneutic of milkweed,
milkweed, in the mind of Joseph, sitting beside milkweed
near the path, dream-taxonomist, sizzling
eye-balcony in the electron microscope theatre
—milkweed is the campaigns of Alexander into India.'

Hell, we don't even get much milkweed.

That true Dionysian world is set in opposition to the world of Apollo, reason, science and representation, the world that allegedly destroyed Riel, engendered Canada's original sin and brought death into our world and all our woe. In *Assiniboia*, Riel asks one of the characters, 'Who won?' He is told: 'Jansenists, Port Royalists,/Cartesians, Baconians, British empiricists', and 'utilitarians'. Lilburn is still therefore very much writing in the shadow of *The Cloud of Unknowing*, the mystical Catholic treatise on 'the negative way', which proposes that God, and the nature of being, are so far beyond human reason that the only way it can be approached is by appreciating through the senses all that it isn't. He sees humans, and human reason in particular, as set in opposition to the natural order, a grand illusion that has to be overcome.

Besides being a bit much to swallow after Descartes and Bacon, not to mention Copernicus, Galileo and Einstein, this disparaging of human reason veers occasionally into an ugly kind of animist misanthropy. Nature might 'not be the sign of something else' and so shouldn't have the human imposed upon it, but apparently poplar trees can be ventriloquized by Lilburn to say:

> 'The stupid pricks,
> Those people should be buried with fire,
> Let those Canadians, let them be dug in at a small slant,
> Or slivered into the dorsal wall of a church,
> Now and then again later be buried
> With smoking logs tied to them'

Now compare this small-souled, radicalized negative way with that of another native of Saskatchewan, Karen Solie, who in her poem 'An Acolyte Reads The Cloud of Unknowing' has managed to reconcile humans and nature. She infuses the insufficiency of human reason with a deep respect and pathos for it, in the image of 'the man shouting on the steps of the drop-in centre' who 'appears, as much as anyone could, to be hero-ically/wrestling himself free from reality, his pain the soul's/pain in knowing it exists.'

Unintended, self-discrediting irony is *Assiniboia*'s undoing. Lilburn's attempts to strip human illusion from reality only end up occluding it. It's also a bit rich to prescribe as the balm for our colonial wound a nebulous Catholic mysticism whose eschatological esurience played no small part in colonialism, never mind the fact that here it's gussied up as a masque, a poetic form historically performed at court to celebrate some noble occasion. And his revulsion of 'bloodless utilitarianism' doth protest too much; I can't think of a poet writing today whose style is more subservient to functionality. Ultimately, the book's Dionysian spirit is sabotaged by all the Apollonian talk that insists it's good for us.

ANNE CARSON

'To live past the end of your myth is a perilous thing' warns the jacket copy of Anne Carson's fourteenth book, *Red Doc>*, a sequel to her 1998 novel-in-verse *Autobiography of Red*. The myth in question is that of the red monster Geryon and his murderer Herakles, which Carson reinvented as a love story in *Autobiography of Red*. *Red Doc>* finds them years later, living under different names (Geryon is now simply G, and Herakles may or may not be the former soldier suffering from PTSD named, actually, Sad). Their story has advanced beyond the mythic gantry of Steisichorus that underpinned *Autobiography of Red*—they're in uncharted territory. But that dust jacket injunction is courting a kind of peril for Carson herself, where it stands in the place that hyperbolic platitudes, like this one from Michael Ondaatje, used to occupy: 'Anne Carson is, for me, the most exciting poet writing in English today.'

Is it really possible to still think that? Whereas Carson's work in translation has remained fresh and vital, the original work has lost its irreverence, its charm, its dashed-off erudition, weird lists and stand-up essays. The attraction so many people, especially young people, feel when reading Carson has to do I think with her stern but casual diction, its feeling of being both learned and dressed-down, affectless and brimming with feeling, like sensing someone smiling behind a mask. *Red Doc>* is ponderous and po-faced, and prodigiously spendthrift with its publisher's supply of paper, setting the poem in a two-inch, centre-justified column. The only justification for this I can come up with, after some thinking about it, is that if the columns had been four inches wide instead of two, the book would have been only 82 pages long, instead of the more Carson-esque 164.

In other words this poem, like so many of Carson's, has no formal meaning. Its shape, how its lines are broken, is arbitrary. Nothing would be lost, save the existence of a small forest, if Carson had changed her line length. A similar thing is happening with her zany punctuation. Carson adores a run-on sentence; I don't think there's a single comma in the book. So you get lots and lots of this sort of thing:

> Sexual
>
> situations yes the haste
>
> and ramming yes the hot
>
> cold amazing difference
>
> between before and after
>
> as if a diagram shot inside
>
> out he remembers the
>
> diagram but the feelings
>
> no. Necessity no. One
>
> night under the overpass
>
> they'd got the sex whiff
>
> again.

This isn't really poetry. It's prose—in my opinion, not super-good prose—rammed, if you will, into the pre-set vase of a .doc document. The language is styled according to fashion, not function.

And that fashion is often difficult. It's hard to tell what's going on most of the time in *Red Doc>*; the couple is introduced by a friend, there's a road trip, and G's mother dies in the end. But Carson's difficulty—the threadbare plotting, unindividuated characters and discourteously punctuated sentences—

happens to be the kind of difficulty that makes the writer's job easier. Its elisions lend an aura of mystery to the proceedings, when the only mystery is what's actually happening—which isn't much. And peppered throughout are crisp, sonorous and entirely meaningless aphorisms: 'Motion is part of listening'; 'Between us and animals is a namelessness.' Catnip for the credulous.

The book's most dubious trick is when Carson, sensing her reader on the nod, drops a highfalutin literary reference to intimidate the reader awake. Every now and again we find G 'thinking about Proust to pass the time' or 'dreaming of Daniil Kharms'. Jason Guriel, in his exceptional review of *Red Doc>* in *Poetry* magazine, asks: 'To what extent is Proust—or Beckett, or whomever a Carson book recruits—an interchangeable signifier of hefty, high culture?' The intertext is décor, pure name-dropping never engaged with at any real depth. Its sole function is to bootstrap prestige to writing which never has to earn it for itself.

I'd argue, too, that it's more than a borrowed medal pinned to a threadbare lapel; it's also a bulletproof vest. If you want to reach your verdict on me, it seems to say, you need to pierce through this and this and this. But a knowledge of the referenced authors does nothing to endear the reader to *Red Doc>*, which like all poems lives (or, in this case, dies) by its domestic, rather than imported, merits.

'Poor Marcel,' Carson writes: 'What is there to know.'

Why doesn't Lazarus talk about death? In the moments before his raising in St. John's Gospel, a crowd of loved ones surround his tomb, excoriating Jesus for not being present just before his death, where surely he, the great healer who can make the blind see, could have saved their beloved Lazarus. And then there's the deliciously real moment when Jesus booms, 'remove the stone' and Martha, the dead man's sister, protests that, 'by this time there will be a stench, for he has been dead four days.' Everything after 'Lazarus come forth' is terrifyingly underwritten. We know that 'the man who had died came forth', which to my ear reads more than a bit understated, and that he was 'bound hand and foot with wrappings'. But how did he come forth? Is he hopping or shimmying? Does he, in fact, stink? Then, after Jesus' order to 'unbind him and let him go' the author goes straight into the political ramifications of Lazarus's raising, and how pissed Caiaphas and the Pharisees are about the whole deal.

Didn't anybody ask Lazarus what death was like? Why doesn't the author want to exploit this great narrative moment for a bit of didactic cosmology? Is Lazarus even happy to be alive again? The sense we're left with is of a man somehow more silent reanimated than he was in death, walking home dazed with his baffled family, and thinking maybe about how unspeakably weird the very concept of lunch is now.

In his second book, *Gift Horse* (Signal Editions, 2011), Mark Callanan is St. John's Lazarus. He's even in St. John's. The book was written after a near-fatal bout with meningitis, an infection of the lining of the brain. We get a hint of Callanan's technique in the book's opening poem, 'Butchering Crab' where even though he's 'thinking now/of being halved by forces/ bigger than myself', his thinking of his own death doesn't translate unmitigated to the page. He writes 'none of this/is quite what I meant to say.' But that isn't because he's incapable of saying it. Instead, *Gift Horse* is the newest iteration of an ancient trope: the Orphic injunction not to look back into hell, the amnesiac waters of the river Lethe, and the Trickster of North American First Nation mythology descending eyes-closed for his beloved into the land of the dead. What is it we're told not to do to a gift horse? Look at it.

And so he doesn't, instead employing a series of 'veiled analogies', which through Callanan's incredible command of metaphor, make every irrelevant thing germane to our mortality. In 'Last Suppers' even 'the gas stove/speaks in Pentecostal tongues', and 'the microwave is counting down' to much more than your lunch. In the red-blooded 'Matador', we get something like Callanan's theory of poetics: 'I've learned that setting has no bearing on the scene,/by which I mean event or focal point.' And so when he does something as boring and normal as going shopping, he can infuse the scene with the unspeakable weirdness of being alive and mortal: 'The full-length mirror shows/a child in adult clothes/who wears the stain/of everything he's spilled./I turn in profile. I turn away/and trust that my reflection stays./Who can say where the soul goes?'

In *Gift Horse* the soul goes everywhere, can touch and seize on anything, but its seat is the brain, the organ of the poet's disease and near-death. My grandmother used to tell me that fish is 'brain food' and that eating it would make me smart, and no where in this country has fishing and its absence been more connected to the destiny and genius of a people than in St. John's; Callanan makes that connection over and over. In the spectacular 'Moratorium' he writes, 'And when I say/fishery, I mean the poem itself, the Grand/Bank of versification.' And later he writes: 'when I put codfish in a poem,/it writhes and bucks its body like a fish/out of water, like a fish about to be fried.' It's rare to encounter a poet who can weave economics, wildlife preservation, public policy, personal and civic history, epidemiology and gastronomy together into the tapestry of metaphor using such deceptively simple language.

The collection ends far afield and back in time, with the obliteration of the last wild Newfoundland wolf in 1911. 'Last Seen' is an absolutely incredible poem, which opens on the last surviving member of the species 'mauling a deer under a crab apple tree/in the fall of the year, just as the leaves/began to turn and boil and spill/like organs onto the grass.' As the hunters take aim, 'it was the youngest, the boy, not even/tall as his father, who squeezed the trigger.' Note that the bullet 'broke/the skull at a point just above the muzzle,/tore apart the brain and split/the thoughts into a million fragments.' The poems of *Gift Horse* are those fragments, shored against the poet's ruin. They suggest that when a human being dies, so does a whole species; not just a world view but a world.

AMANDA JERNIGAN

Amanda Jernigan is not Richard Outram.

I mean that neither as insult nor endorsement, though it says something about where you, dear reader, situate yourself in Canadian poetry if you find yourself alternately offended or relieved. It's simply a fact that bears repeating, as the resemblances call out to be enumerated. Jernigan, especially in her debut *Groundwork*, writes what can be called mythopoetry, Canadian poetry's collective revisiting of the golden oldies of Greek and Judeo-Christian mythology, inspired by the lectures and essays of Northrop Frye, and practised, among others, by Richard Outram. Jernigan is one of Outram's finest readers, and even selected and edited *The Essential Richard Outram*, her introduction to which reminds us that one of Outram's recurring characters is a woman named Amanda (others include 'Eden's Adam and Shakespeare's Lear', both of whom recur in Jernigan's poems). Jernigan even intersperses throughout her books the woodcuts of her husband, John Haney, just as Outram did with the woodcuts of his wife, Barbara Howard. Sometimes they write the same. Here are two concluding stanzas, one by Jernigan and one by Outram, from poems they each wrote about Eden's Adam:

You shall find on waking,	Do I wake or sleep? Indeed,
Beyond doubt,	the answer is the same.
Just whether I am breaking	Ask Finnegan. In fact, ask me,
In or out.	if you can guess my name.

Who wrote which? Both somnambulant poems romance a kind of crepuscular uncertainty on the verge of revealing itself, and they do so with remarkably similar rhetorical and formal strategies. Spoiler Alert: on the left is the end of Outram's 'Adam in the Very Act of Love' and on the right is the end of Jernigan's 'The Birds of Paradise' (the name she's goading us to guess, which would be a nice slant rhyme with 'same' and 'name', may very well be 'Outram', the old crypto-trickster).

Maybe the most dispiriting similarity is in the way each has been received by the Canadian poetry world: as niche tastes for philologists within walking distance of the reference library; as poets with enormous intellectual and linguistic resources, but no window, nevermind WiFi; as poets who are ultimately easier to admire than they are to love. *Groundwork*, though it contained some immaculately crafted, sonically beautiful, and almost overwhelmingly considered poems (see 'Aubade', 'Adam's Prayer', 'Exodus' and 'Catch', for example), felt as a whole, with its three-headed mytho-conceits—Heaney-esque archeology, the Pentateuch, and the Odyssey—like a Cerberus of two-too many minds. Though Jernigan writes that her mythic excavations 'laid bare the structure of (her) thinking', and the book's promotional copy proclaims itself a 'reworking of European myth on the order of Yeats's *The Tower*', the book is almost devoid of anything contemporary that could convince the reader that the myths aren't just being rehashed, or rehearsed, but reborn. It's an inheritance without the debit card you need to spend it now.

In her introduction to *The Essential Richard Outram*, Jernigan writes: 'Outram, like Frye, rewrote his central myth again and again over the course of his career. But the idiom in which he rewrote the myth evolved. We can see him moving from the general, to the particular, to the personal.' The same evolution is underway in Jernigan's second book, *All the Daylight Hours*, a book at once more studied and more idiosyncratic. More to the

point, she's gotten better at brain-melting Outramian etymo-
logical flights. Take her 'Ply' for example:

> On deck the tars had leave to talk
> so long as they were spinning. Tale
> and twine were thus entangled: language
> tends to twinning. So tutored
> by his fingers, the yarning sailor knew
> how words, like wool, must be perplexed
> if they're to clothe a truth. At times
> he'd see a skein of seabirds streaming
> towards the spindle, or feel the sea
> itself perplexed as the vessel turned
> to ply, or hear the steersman's wheel
> and know, for all its to's and fro's
> it spoke, in turn, of revolution —
> then would the deck beneath his feet
> seem treadle to the great wheel of the sun.

This is incredibly fine work, the four-foot iambic line itself
being treadled to give the rhythm of a sea shanty,
of a ship at sea and of a garment being sewn. And that ingenious
first 'perplexed', here meaning both 'confused', and 'entwined',
is one of those rare occasions in contemporary poetry where you
can see exactly how moving the exact right word in the exact
right place can be (and for Outramites out there, I hear at least
six distinct meanings of 'Ply' here: one textile, two nautical, and
three behavioural, all interwoven).

At 100 pages, work like this is bound to be few and far
between. Jernigan, like Homer, nods. So what: at 40 kilometres
an hour in a school zone, a Ferrari and a Ford go the same speed.
Jernigan is at her best in *All the Daylight Hours* when she lets

the daylight of today into her work. In 'Poem with the Gift of a Timepiece', Jernigan brings her command of conceit and form to the dedication of a wristwatch, and ends up saying something perfect about imperfection. And in what is I think the most beautiful poem in the book, 'Encounter', we see Jernigan's mythic intellect react to the first ultrasound of her unborn baby, revealing, 'not an astronaut, but Earth,/so "small, light blue, so touchingly alone."/Thus Leonov.' As in Alexy Leonov, the first spacewalker. We're miles above Outram now, but Jernigan ends in a moment he himself would probably have reached for:

> And yet as I beheld you floating there
> I felt myself grow small, the air grow thin,
> as if I were the one adrift in space,
> and you the one who might yet pull me in.

CLIVE JAMES'S DANTE

My most Dantean moment, something as figurative and self-inflicted as anything in the *Inferno*, happened in Dante's house. I was on vacation in Florence with my sister and girlfriend, and needed a day at the city's museums to recover from what was supposed to be a leisurely bike tour of some Tuscan wineries the day before, but turned out to be a series of *hors catégorie* vertical climbs in 40-degree heat punctuated by power carbo-loads and micro-benders.

The old GI tract was in purgatory as we arrived at the Dante house museum, where an officious Florentine in an immaculate uniform and behind bulletproof glass charged us 20 euros each to enter what surely must be the absolute worst museum in the world—three nearly empty rooms with, say, framed posters of contemporary renderings of Dante's Ptolemaic universe, or a couple shabby costumes of what men and women in 14th-century Florence may have worn. Not even a goddamn deathmask.

On our way out, nature called, and the girls said they'd wait for me outside. And so it was something of a piece to discover a little too late that the Dante house museum washroom was—er, *come si dice*, out of *carta igienica*. The girls wouldn't even hear me scream. The sign above hell reads: 'Forget your hopes. They were what brought you here.' Then the Dantean thought entered, both vulgar and full of grace, as I turned my head slowly to my copy of John Ciardi's translation of *The Divine Comedy* sitting beside the sink. Dante wouldn't mind. In fact, I think he'd get it: His house brought it on himself.

And so if, like me, your copy of *The Divine Comedy* has lost some pages over the years, now is a perfect time to invest in Clive

James's landmark new translation of what is surely the greatest poem ever written. James's translation reaffirms Dante's place in the very centre of world literature, and reminds us again of just how much of ourselves, and our time, Dante prefigured.

The first task that one of Dante's English translators has to set himself to is figuring out how to render the outlandish musicality of Dante's terza rima, his interlocking three-line rhyme scheme, into our rather rhyme-poor language. Dante's vernacular Tuscan dialect—which today forms the basis of contemporary Italian because of the immense influence of the poem—makes rhyming, both at the end of the line and throughout it, almost an inevitability. Not so in English. And when English poets take a crack at terza rima, the results are often singsongy in a way Dante's Florentine never is, which is why Robert Pinsky used slant- and half-rhymes in his *Inferno*.

James succeeds as well as any translator in the last hundred years at conveying Dante's *sprezzatura*, his sense of propulsion and hyper-concision, and he does this by eschewing the terza rima for the four-line rhyming quatrain, which admirably conveys the paradoxical sound of Dante's music, and its implication for human destiny, its being both bound by a fractal formal structure, and free to flex its animal muscularity. Here's how he renders the famous Paolo and Francesca moment:

> But then the moment came we turned a page
> And all our powers of resistance failed:
> When we read of that great knight in a rage
> To kiss the smile he so desired, Paolo,
> This one so quiet now, made my mouth still —
> Which, loosened by those words, had trembled so —
> With his mouth. And right then we lost the will —
> For love can will will's loss, as well you know.

But James's success can't help but remind readers of the absurdity of translating a poet as colossal as Dante. Imagine, for example, what the poor bastards in Florence must be getting when an accomplished elder poet translates Shakespeare into his native Italian. Dante is the sort of poet whose superhuman talents once led Erich Auerbach, maybe the greatest literary critic of the twentieth century, to spend 500 words parsing Dante's use of the words '*Allor surse*', which is a very nuanced, very beautiful way of saying 'and then'.

But James, like Dante himself, is a trickster who's stolen something essential and life-giving from the dark, ensuring that commerce is occurring across the border between the sacred and the profane. His translation should be an occasion for the literary world to reconsider just how much of our own minds he invented.

What did Dante invent? He invented conceptualism; the idea of his book, and how it's executed, is so brilliant that it predates by some 700 years Kenneth Goldsmith's formulation that the best books are so good you don't need to read them. *The Divine Comedy* is unlike any other poem in that its architecture alone is enough to make it famous; three books, or canticles, in the three realms of the afterlife, each containing thirty-three poems, each poem of which is composed of interlocking three-line stanzas, all pointing to the perfection of the triune god's design. He prefigures the defining feature of postmodernism, the commingling of the high and low. For centuries scandalized commentators didn't know what to do with Dante, who could marry the classical and the contemporary, who would dare debase the epic form by writing it in a vulgar vernacular, and pay equal attention to the afterlives of both the Virgin Mary and his political enemies.

He revels in gossip, the comeback imagined too late. *High*

Fidelity curatorial taste-making, and the essential, divine judgement of *The Voice* and *The Bachelorette*.

The most beautiful thing about Dante, though, is not that he brought the afterlife to earth, but that he smuggled earth into the afterlife. Virgil, his literary idol, takes him through hell and purgatory, but his guide into heaven is Beatrice, a Florentine girl Dante saw once in church, and fell in love with. The two may never have spoken in life—she died young and Dante died much later in exile from his beloved Florence—but in her he invented literary realism. She haunted his life, his poems, his dreams, and he gave her the exalted seat in his masterpiece, humanity's masterpiece, what the author simply called *The Comedy*, something too sacred to devote to the divine.

DAVID SEYMOUR

David Seymour's biographical note from his first book read that he 'photo-doubled for Russell Crowe'. There could be no better preparation for a poet. It's exactly what Eliot had in mind, when he wrote that the 'progress of an artist is a continual self-sacrifice, a continual extinction of personality.' If done right, with artifice, a little luck, and a good director of photography, the extinction is so complete that the poet's very head, the wellspring of his poems, is transformed into, say, the unknockoutable noggin of James Braddock in the disabusing lie that is *Cinderella Man*.

'Nothing would verify the cleanliness/and newly refined balance of this space/quite so thoroughly as my absence,' Seymour writes in his aptly titled second collection, *For Display Purposes Only*, a quantum leap in his development. Where his first book was brimming with promise, but overlong, and overweight, *For Display Purposes Only* is fighting trim, and poem after poem is a knockout blow.

The title should alert readers to the fact that Seymour's poems are self-consciously artificial products with designs on our desires. His poetry's paradoxical twin concerns are doubling and impersonality. In the opening poem, 'Wild Lines', we get snapshots of Seymour's domestic life: 'There goes the apartment performing/accurate impersonations of itself.' But the photographer is always a mystery: 'Our side of the camera I can't recall with detail.' Like a fast-food-commercial makeup artist, or a poet, Seymour offers dishes that, in their manufactured perfection, stoke our hunger for their living referent, but can't by that same virtue ever satisfy it.

It's all very Platonic, and sometimes we can sense that Seymour is disturbed by a living art's inferiority to life. In 'Eyewitness Testimony', a sort of police procedural in quatrains, facts and linguistic flights become disturbingly indistinguishable:

Earlier, from the precipitate sky, hail the size
of golf balls pelted the clubhouse. Errant
hail-sized golf balls shanked the clubhouse
before the golfers ran for cover from the weather.

By the end of 'Eyewitness Testimony' we're no closer to solving the crime. Nor should we be; however beautiful it is, a poem is a terrible way to solve a murder. That tension between art and life is further troubled in Seymour's lovely 'Clone', where he plays out the thought experiment we all have had, of creating clones of ourselves so that we're free for aesthetics, to 'learn to play guitar' or 'finally fangle origami'. But something essentially ourselves is lost when we're only art. Seymour writes:

I'll hit the town and rake the coals they've left. I am
going to wear my favourite shirt, the brown one. Or am I.

But at other times Seymour can't seem to believe that we're only real, and not only aesthetic. He writes—spectacularly—of a group of people 'griping toward the door,/their bodies to their lives as water is to waves.'

Seymour navigates this complicated dialectic through a tour-de-force reimagining of the formal repertoire. The closing poem 'Zero Kelvin' is so clever and sonically alert—with lines like 'Gentle patriots of the suburbs whose faith/is an acronym for fibre access in the home'—that I didn't even recognize it as a sonnet my first time through. The traditional Anglo-Saxon caesura is reimagined as the pause between news bulletins in BBC World News. The list poem, the monologue, the ekphrastic, the prose poem—all are deftly disguised in Seymour's new costuming.

Maybe weirdest and most beautiful of all is the series, interspersed throughout the collection, of the opening pages of various imaginary genre novels, complete with page number—always '1'—and title—'A Modest Sum' or 'Cory on the Bash Awhile'. From boozy Scottish brogue to hard-boiled detectivese, Seymour proves himself to be an immensely gifted character writer in these bizarre, abrupt narrative non sequiturs. But what's their point? What purpose do they serve?

In 'The Photo Double', Seymour writes that acting hurt 'has less to do with feeling pain/than understanding timing.' What makes *For Display Purposes Only* such a powerful work of art is how deeply it believes that. Poetry is performance; art is artifice. And it's essentially entertainment. When it works, it's not because its Romantic soul spelunking was to a record depth, or because its confessionalist moral laundering was the most Tide Fresh. It's because its maker believes enough in what's real to wander off and master what's artificial. Or put another way: the true poet isn't someone who's found his voice, but someone who's lost it.

Joshua Mehigan is one of the few living poets unfashionable enough to still be writing poems. He didn't get the memo. While his contemporaries have been busy fine-tuning their algorithms, tweaking their genomes, and re-mystifying their obscurantisms, Mehigan has been perfecting his lucid, plain-spoken ear worms. His second book, *Accepting the Disaster*, is the most generous, deeply felt, and technically ingenious collection to appear in English in years.

As the title suggests, the author of *Accepting the Disaster* has taken Samuel Beckett's advice to young writers to heart: 'Despair young and never look back.' Mehigan's world is populated by the overworked and underemployed, the sort of people who can sum up people: 'No one is special. We grow old. We die.' But before that, there's work to be done, at 'The Smokestack', which 'was older than stop signs, / It would always be there', or 'The Cement Plant':

> The thing was blind to all its own ends
> but the one. Men's ordinary lives,
> measured out on a scale alien
> to that on which its life was measured,
> were spent in crawling the junk machine,
> fitting new gaskets, screws, and bearings,
> deceiving it toward the mood required
> for it to avail and pay. Somehow
> it did. None cheered it. It sustained them.

Home from the factory, after a worker 'ate his cube steak

and drank his milk', he'll dream of work in 'Dream Job', then wake to return to it. Philip Larkin, who famously crowed 'deprivation is to me what daffodils were to Wordsworth', would be impressed with Mehigan, who can write an exquisite psalm to the fundamental attributional error:

> Grant me, Lord, the wretchedness
> to attribute each success
> wrung from air with strength and skill
> to your paranormal will
>
> and to credit grief, disease,
> poverty, catastrophes,
> shortfall, pain, and death alone
> to some failing of my own.

For Mehigan, 'life, this passing unendurable fever', is 'a world of pain, a glint of joy'. That glint of joy is art, poetry's ability to both re-create and redress the insults and depredations of a world that doesn't much care for us. In the book's centrepiece, a sixteen-page ballad called 'The Orange Bottler', Mehigan takes us into the mind of a mentally ill man who stops taking his antipsychotics. '"Don't take me!" cried the clozapine./ "Don't take me!" cried the pill./By ten he was feeling restless,/with a whole day left to kill.' Where lesser poets would use the subject matter as license to wallow into the brackish logorrhoea of Gertrude Stein, Mehigan does the opposite, deploying the singsong rhymes of the ballad form as an analogue for the specious meaning-making of schizophrenia:

> Why should he go to his workplace?
> Who was his supervisor?

He had a sickening feeling
that he was becoming wiser.

His room filled up with interest.
He had begun to think!
He thought of the knives in the kitchen
and the bottles under the sink.

Mehigan has written brilliantly about his own battles with mental illness in an essay for *Poetry* magazine (where many of these poems, including 'The Orange Bottle', first appeared). 'Face to face, if I trust you,' he wrote, 'I'm rambling and far too open. Impulse control is a problem. I've deliberately avoided this mode in my writing. At least there I have the power of revision.' Mehigan therefore represents a vital alternative to the canard that the only way to faithfully represent the messiness of contemporary life is with messy writing, the pseudo-profundity of the self-indulgently obtuse, a pathologically American *idée fixe* that's dominated the last hundred years of poetic thinking and can be traced from T. S. Eliot through Gertrude Stein, John Ashbery and so many MFA theses. 'Because forethought and discretion rarely appear in my personal life,' Mehigan writes, 'I like to cultivate them in my poems.' It's precisely because Mehigan is so well acquainted with disaster and disorder that he records them so painstakingly and precisely, according them the memorability they deserve.

In the title poem, a litany of catastrophes piles its plurals up, accumulating like a coastal shelf:

The NGOs and global censuses
found that in wars and fatal illnesses
half the world ranked above world averages.

Millions succumbed to downlevel viruses,
millions to food and water shortages.
The west wind throbbed with doleful cadences,
salats, psalms, mantras, sutras, kaddishes.

By the time we notice that nearly every line ends in 'es', the trick is already sprung: the disaster is our world, and like only the best poets, Mehigan makes it most convincingly natural when he tames the chaos with technique. And the proof of Mehigan's accomplishment is that even when his poems are their most formal, scanning and rhyming perfectly, they're also their most organic and colloquial. Ultimately, though, the enduring value of *Accepting the Disaster* is in the lines and poems that are impossible to forget: 'Of darkness, there was only ever one kind,/and our pupils grew in it and eclipsed our irises.' 'Whether pain looks more like death or life/depends upon your personal preferences.' And every syllable of 'Believe it', an instant classic:

Hard to believe that, after all of it,
in bed for good now, knowing you haven't done
one thing of any lasting benefit
or grasped how to be happy, or had fun,

you must surrender everything and pass
into a new condition that is not
night, or a country, or a sleep, or peace,
but nothing, ever anymore, for you.

Accepting the Disaster is the closest thing to a masterpiece a reader of contemporary poetry is likely to encounter.

When, in high school, I briefly took a comedy class at Second City, our teacher got right to it and explained how jokes work: 'Working from the Lacanian idea of the *point de capiton* or quilting point, the idea that meaning is retroactively determined by the final word in a statement, Alenka Zupančič frames the punch line in terms of this Lacanian operation.' JK—no, that was written by Ryan Fitzpatrick and Jonathan Ball, in their introduction to *Why Poetry Sucks: An Anthology of Humorous Experimental Canadian Poetry*, an essay that I'm confident is the least funny thing ever written about what makes things funny. There's only one rule in comedy and every comic knows it: never explain your jokes using Lacanian psychoanalytic theory and/or Baltic post-structuralism. You should sooner try getting turned on listening to an artificially intelligent garburator explain the mechanics of oral sex—in German.

In its best Jerry Seinfeld impression, the world asks: 'What's the deal with poetry?' Fitzpatrick and Ball respond: 'No literary genre appears less funny than poetry, where conventional wisdom has it that a "good poem" must move the reader to some epiphany through the subtle revelation of some aspect of the human condition.' Here are all the experimental type's old bogeymen aligned and arraigned in a single class action: not just wisdom, but conventional wisdom, 'good poems', readers, epiphanies, the human condition, subtlety, and revelations, which when we're talking about comedy, we might call punch lines. To the rescue is a mixed bag of poets that Fitzpatrick and Ball have decided are 'experimental', an adjective that when sandwiched between 'humorous' and 'poetry' is more indictment than endorsement. Ladies and germs, strap on the Depends and welcome to the stage Dorothy Trujillo Lusk with 'Vulgar Marxism':

After past retrieval
Justly apt shrinkage and drunkardliness
shoulder values
party lapses—animalian floral techtronics
sheet apropos goof
aspirate
PUNK SNOUT in LINSEY WOOLIES
FINAGLIN' the DULL FINKDOWN MAN—
HOLE
SPECIES washing up of coastal waters—each shivery
Aside binding co-determinate froth management.

If you found that funny, I bet it's not for the reasons Lusk intended. If you didn't laugh, you DULL FINKDOWN MAN you, Fitzpatrick and Ball can jump in and explain to you why you should have: 'Lusk resists the transparency of language (the idea that language can or should attempt to clearly transmit meaning to its listener).' Get it? I'd submit that it's hard to be funny—at least on purpose—when you're succeeding this well at not making sense.

It's worth wondering why experimental poets would want to be considered funny at all. Fitzpatrick and Ball ask a question that may be too old-fashioned for two young lions of the avant-garde: 'If comedy can't win an Oscar, how will it ever win the Griffin?' Less interesting than their transparent desire for such a traditional, mainstream accolade as a Griffin Prize is the fact that Fitzpatrick and Ball implicitly recognize that comedy is our culture's dominant mode of discourse. Our George Orwell is Jon

Stewart; our Samuel Beckett is Louis C.K. Young writers of talent who want to interrogate social and aesthetic values don't want to be Gertrude Stein; they want to be Tina Fey.

But what makes humour work—how to elicit the laugh that's utterly immune to explicative theory—is diametrically opposed to what unites many of the experimental poets in *Why Poetry Sucks*, a suspicion of meaning-making. With the bathwater of form went the baby of sense. But Fitzpatrick and Ball try to square the circle with—you guessed it—theory. 'Both the joke and poetry,' they argue by way of Viktor Shklovsky, operate 'by making our language and our social operations *strange*. Thus, defamiliarization is, arguably, the basic gesture of poetry.' Both poetry and humour 'estrange us from language and its transparent, communicative capacity.' Some poetry, maybe, but never jokes, which are as likely to elicit a laugh this way as would a tickler who doesn't believe in touch.

The exceptions prove the rule, and instructively. Whereas most of the poets in *Why Poetry Sucks* are too arch to be anything but droll, the poets who are actually funny are those whose poems don't cleave quite so programmatically—I'm tempted to write 'traditionally'—to the high-minded self-seriousness of the avant-garde. Echoing the deliciously mean advice of Christopher Hitchens, who said that a joke should always be at someone's expense, Gregory Betts has a clutch of poems compiling the accidental genius of his undergraduate students' essays: 'Canadians are victimized by having to fight Margaret Atwood for survival.' Dina Del Bucchia has a self-help poem called 'How to be Angry', a 'rage meditation', which advises: 'Clear your throat to be heard/above the Food Network reruns./Julia Child's breasts and apron almost/touching, her voice, reverberating from/beyond the grave, reaches its highest/octave of instruction, *Marinate the quail!*'

But it's the inclusion of David McGimpsey, the only contributor who also happens to be both a stand-up comic and sonneteer, that discredits the intellectual gymnastics of the anthologists. By far the funniest poet in the anthology, he also happens to be something of a formalist, and one suspicious of the leftist high-mindedness that franchises so much of the avant-garde's sententious humourlessness. In 'My Life as a Canadian Writer', he writes (in near-perfect blank verse, too): 'I learned the beauty of socialism/from writers so passionate they'd cry/when they didn't get a grant. We'd go north/and laugh at the thought of Alden Nowlan.' On its own terms and without the help of Continental theorists, it's funny, grammatical and it scans. For Fitzpatrick and Ball, that sucks.

Victorians had marriage plots; we have the end of the world. Over the last hundred years, the post-apocalyptic genre has slowly but inexorably supplanted social realism as the dominant artistic genre of our time, beginning with Eliot's *The Waste Land* and culminating in *The Walking Dead*. We've come by the nightmares honestly, the century having offered up the grist of two world wars, nuclear weaponry, and aerosolized superbugs on super-jumbo airbuses. But more than the hydrogen bomb or Ebola, the horror most responsible for the ascendancy of post-apocalyptic art is the assembly line. By dividing up labour in the modern world, the assembly line sustains civilization, making us each experts of a single widget in a wider clockwork we can afford to be ignorant of. Thanks to Henry Ford, come Armageddon no one of us can put the world together again.

Edmonton-born poet Sarah Lang channels the impotence and ignorance of late capitalism in her second collection *For Tamara*. Set in a world decimated by nuclear war, the book is a prose poem written as a mother's survival guide for her daughter. 'Before this your mother was a writer', confesses the unnamed narrator, which, as the mushroom clouds rose, immediately rendered her and her peers the least useful human beings on Earth. Horrifyingly she adds, 'now she is a doctor and a teacher', making it hard not to recall Nikita Khrushchev's quip that in a nuclear winter 'the living will envy the dead'.

For Tamara is a compendium of advice ('eat eggplant, it's good for you') and DIY factoids ('poplar trees have sunscreen [SPF15] on the south side') interspersed with lamentations for a lost world ('I wish you could watch ST:TNG') and the poetry of a mother speaking plainly to her daughter ('Mum wishes she could have a glass of wine'), with some hand-drawn and fashionably illegible illustrations thrown in. The tone is provisional and scattered, as if the book was written in the stolen moments between makeshift amputations. The scant exposition the book offers suggests that the narrator is the leader of a group of haggard survivors living somewhere in North America, running a self-sustaining farm, hospital and school.

The book's mix of poetry and practical advice brings to mind, oddly, Virgil's *Georgics*, which tutors its reader on how to plant crops, till soil and keep bees while digressing beautifully on myth and history—a poem disguised as a manual. The real lesson in the *Georgics*, however, is how it adheres to Horace's maxim that poetry should 'delight and instruct', the idea being that it's easier to remember something useful when it's memorably stated. *Georgics* endured not because of its sagacity—Virgil thought that bee colonies are formed in the eviscerated corpse of a cow—but by its memorability. Here's how William Logan put it: 'Don't think what you have to say is important. The way you say it is what's important. What you have to say is rubbish.'

The wisdom offered in *For Tamara* has its mnemonic moments ('Eat and sleep regularly./The end of the world will be there tomorrow') and is sometimes enormously useful ('soak hardwood ash in water to make lye'). But beyond the fascination of the subject, the poem as a poem delights far less than I hoped it would, and can't be saved by its smattering of factoids. *For Tamara* is too often lackadaisical, formulaic and repetitive, the writing unmusical and quickly forgotten. A typical formulation is a two- or three-part paragraph of advice quick cut to clichéd fawning, like: 'Thyroid meds./I'm so proud of you.' Sometimes the clichés are so saccharine as to be cavity causing, like 'Love someone for who they are', or 'God, you make me so proud, you have no idea' or 'Of course I miss your Dad. Like you wouldn't believe.' This is the nostalgic, uncomplicated sound of being spoken to as a child, the palliative language of cliché and euphemism one has to outgrow in order to survive as an adult.

I hold the book in my hand and try to imagine it was written for me, and then the questions come. Why in a world so short on ink did Mom insert her own innumerable forward slashes into every single line? What secret message was Mom encoding by over-punctuating a perfectly serviceable sentence like 'When you cut down a tree./Let it dry./For good firewood'? How could someone who crossed the bright demarcation between civilization and apocalypse, a self-taught surgeon who has amputated countless gangrenous arms write something like, 'I can write this book because I have never seen time as linear'? Why didn't she draw the maps so that I could read them?

The book provides a kind of answer: 'T., as a kid I used to talk to myself on my way to school./Writing this book has me doing this again.' In other words, this isn't really for you, kiddo: it's for me. Ultimately, with its formulaic affection, its arty punctuation, its coolly inscrutable maps and diagrams, *For Tamara* feels too much like the newest poem to roll off a hale poetry culture's production line, and not enough like the last will and testament of a survivor too grizzled by the apocalypse to allow herself—and her helpless child—that kind of artful indulgence.

DAVID McGIMPSEY

In discussing the work of David McGimpsey, it's worth remembering the curious enthusiasm William Wordsworth captured in his sonnet 'Composed upon Westminster Bridge, September 3, 1802'. Why? Because Wordsworth could look at the city of London—the symbol of humanity's excommunication from universal nature and therefore from happiness—and call it beautiful: 'Earth has not anything to show more fair:/Dull would he be of soul who could pass by/A sight so touching in its majesty:/This City…'

One can imagine the knowing elbowings his fellow Romantics must have exchanged when Wordsworth wrote about the filthy, polluted Thames: 'The river glideth at its own sweet will.' So too are you likely to hear snickering about David McGimpsey's triumphant new collection of poems, *Li'l Bastard* (Coach House Books), as when he writes from Montreal ('where both coffee and café are overpriced/and served with a distinctive Euro-sass') that:

> The river speaks to me in TV themes:
> Join the wacky St. Lawrence and the gang
> for laffs a-plenty in La Belle Province.

David McGimpsey is one of the few living poets who can make the same claim as Terence, the comic playwright of the 2nd century BC: 'I am a human; no human thing is alien to me.' He is a ravenous and democratic consumer of the things we make; hamburgers, Bud, impractical cars, television series, sports, Miltonic elegies, and yes, overpriced coffee, all find equal footing in his work. Nothing we do is alien to him. His poems, which are often classically formal tributes to pop cultural products, made a lot of critics uncomfortable. What did McGimpsey really think about Alan Hale, the skipper from Gilligan's Island, about whom he wrote an ostensibly fulsome elegy in the style of Tennyson, in his debut, *Lard Cake*? Are we in on the joke or the butt of it?

The first thing you notice about McGimpsey's new book is that it's a squat little bastard. It's about an inch shorter than the standard Coach House book of poetry. Even in this we can hear anxieties about 'high art'. And at 152 pages, it hasn't quite watched its weight. But what else could we expect from a book so shamelessly enamoured with fast food? Contained within are '128 Chubby Sonnets'—sixteen-line poems McGimpsey has been perfecting throughout his career that indulge themselves two extra lines.

The book takes the form of a picaresque, a spiritual and geographical road trip with both Saul Bellow and John Berryman as back-seat drivers. In *Li'l Bastard* we journey with McGimpsey from 'the unreachable squalor of (his) home' in Montreal to Texas, television (in the 1970s detective serial *Barnaby Jones*), Illinois, Nashville, L.A. and back to Montreal, stopping at taco stands, local watering holes, palaces, airports and MFA classrooms along the way. The rapaciousness of the book's affairs engenders the 'bastard' of the title: The poems are unfranchised amalgams that are no less natural for their illegitimacy.

In McGimpsey, high culture and low culture can interbreed because they simply are; whereas most poets write prescriptively, sticking to subjects deemed respectably poetic, McGimpsey writes descriptively, singing the world as it actually is. Musing on the palace of Versailles (and the Place Versailles, a mall in his hometown of Ville D'Anjou, where gaudy imitations of the former preside) and wondering if the fountains are more 'Aztec in influence, or perhaps Bauhaus' we experience the sudden eruption of 'Snooki getting punched by that dude at Karma'. McGimpsey shows us that all Western decadence—from imperial France to the Jersey shore—is equally delicious, strange and just simply there.

But if both the high and low are valid in McGimpsey's poetry, middle culture is the only evil (an interesting course of study would be to examine how the cultural middle is connected to the physiological middle, where we gain our weight). Part of 'the unspeakable beauty of it all' in this book is how much of a triumph over the easy irony of post-modernism it really is. Early on we get this brilliant encounter:

> 'Who're you calling a literary hipster?'
> he huffed, putting down his pint of Steam Whistle.
> I apologized, of course, and promised
> to read his second book, Suck It, Dick Cheney.

The one thing McGimpsey can't abide is the facile Canadianism of the leftist provincial contrarian, defining himself against all things American and hegemonic. Indeed, we realize over the course of *Li'l Bastard* how misguided and empty the dominant narrative of Canadian nationalism really is. In 'My life as a Canadian Writer' he writes:

> My first short story, 'The Provincial Fair',
> was rejected twenty-five times before
> it found its home in the Muskoka Review.
> From then on it's all been smooth sailing.

Nothing is uglier than the unscrupulous canonization of the quaint and uncomplicated. McGimpsey's vision will be uncomfortable to many, because it's a continental vision; It requires us to accept that the American imports we grew up with—televised, advertised, digitized—are as much our intellectual birthright as the self-excoriating isolationism we were told was good for us, and were forced to eat before we could leave the table and play. But it is a vision of the highest order, a truly inclusive and scrupulous feast, caloric, chaotic and free.

MICHAEL ROBBINS

Michael Robbins is the rarest kind of poet: one who wakes up famous one morning (wait, I'm still going) before his first book is even out. When his poem 'Alien vs. Predator' appeared in *The New Yorker* in January 2009, it went, well, sort of viral. Music critics Carl Wilson and Sasha Frere-Jones gushed about it on their blogs. *The Village Voice* ran a three-page interview with Robbins about his 20-line poem. *Gothamist* recommended him for the Nobel Prize (Freud said there are no jokes).

What made 'Alien vs. Predator' so attractive to so many people—and not only the sort of people who write poems—wasn't just that he called Rilke a jerk and an elk a dick, or that he boasted irresistibly that 'I translate the Bible into velociraptor', though there was pleasure to be had in seeing something so unabashedly twisted in the white-shoe *New Yorker*. What his many fans responded to, even if it was working on a pre-conscious part of their brains, was recognizing—finally!—the familiar, menacing voice of late capitalism itself in our poetry.

In April 2012, Penguin published Robbins's first collection, which takes its name from the poem that made him famous. *Alien vs. Predator* is one of the most anticipated collections of poetry in recent memory and I'm happy to report it lives up to the hype, and then some. The book opens with the *Duino Elegies* quotation from Rilke, 'the jerk': 'Praise this world'. And so he does; in Robbins's poems dancehall king Buju Banton shares space with John Milton, who 'jumps out of my birthday cake'. Forrest Gump and Rihanna are as likely to be ventriloquized as Whitman or Roethke. Bulls--t passes as fact. Profanity and profundity rhyme. Exquisitely crafted sonnets channel-surf tone and subject line by line. If John Ashbery and David McGimpsey have proven that popular culture is a suitable subject for poetry, Robbins goes a step further and attempts its formal mimesis.

And he does it really goddamn well. A typical Robbins poem borrows from Frederick Seidel the moral terror that formal rigour and rhyme can inspire. He short-circuits that with a technique Paul Muldoon showcased in his poem 'Symposium', where clichés are cut up and spliced together. But it isn't just clichés that Robbins cross-wires; he puts all of our culture into remixed conversation, and coins some hilariously subversive phrases along the way. The Joy Division lyric becomes 'Love will tear us a new a—hole'. Freud's alibi and a lullaby round transform into 'Life is but the interpretation of a dream/Gently, gently down the drain.' He rhymes 'scorpion' with 'Jack Kevorkian'; 'Axl' (of Guns N' Roses) with 'Paxil'; 'Stegasaur' with 'megastore'. One of the poems, 'Enjoy My Symptom', takes its title from Slavoj Žižek, who writes:

A short circuit occurs when there is a faulty connection in the network—faulty, of course, from the standpoint of the network's smooth functioning.... Is not one of the most effective critical procedures to cross wires that do not usually touch?

What makes *Alien vs. Predator* so interesting is that he makes us realize the voice of the contemporary muse is the same as the scopophilic inner voice of the good consumer, screaming 'buy buy buy' at everything we see. In Robbins's poetry, the software of the free market, where everything is for sale, is run on the horrifically decadent hardware of Western thinking, where everything is in its right place.

Alien vs. Predator is neither doe-eyed endorsement of capitalism nor #occupy ipso facto censure; it simply sings its fact. In

'Lust for Life' Robbins writes: 'The truth gets me hard. Song selection/is key.' In a beautiful and brilliant review of Seidel that Robbins wrote for the *London Review of Books*, Robbins relates a bit of a botched interview he did with the great Phallus Man of American poetry where he asks Seidel what the function of poetry is in contemporary society:

Seidel simply responded with Samuel Johnson's line, borrowed from Sidney (who got it from Horace), that poetry must please and instruct. Fair enough: so what are his poems instructing us? 'That's for you to say.'

Robbins's own work is equally resistant to the portable moral, and that's what makes it vital. Like capitalism itself, its pleasures conspire against its hideousness. In order to reckon with Robbins, we as readers have to reckon with the whole meretricious socio-economic structure in which we're entangled.

But how in Adam Smith's name can you not adore a poet who ends his first book with:

> I take this cadence from the spinning plates
> where the DJ plots the needle's fall.
> I take it, and I give it back again
> to the dollar dollar bill and the yes yes y'all.

STEVIE HOWELL

To the Southern Ontario kid raised on Fox 29's down-market commercials, who can pronounce a Fuccillo 'huge' and can sing the Cellino & Barnes jingle by heart, there's a particular kind of innocence that's lost when you first visit Buffalo. In her debut, Stevie Howell puts her finger on the feeling, shocked to find that although it had sent its advertisements as emissaries, 'the whole city was shuttered, not even for sale.'

The lines are from Howell's 'A Sketch', and, as is often the case in her poems, stowed away in disabuse is abuse; the trip to Buffalo is led by Howell's high-school 'life-drawing teacher' who is preying upon the art students in his charge, 'his panting for your teen-ness/steaming up his windshield'. At the Albright-Knox museum, Howell isn't taken by the artwork: 'their synthetic stillness/recalled poised hunting decoys, and it seemed I had/the senses of a Mallard.' Like the duck being aped, and with an ear for the menacing double-entendre of the 'life-drawing teacher', Howell 'can see … the seams/from the casting mould', and spots the mendacious knock-off. 'I wasn't conned,' she crows.

Howell is so ambivalent about the redemptive power of art that she's named her debut collection of poems after a word you can't even spell, never mind pronounce—the Egyptian hieroglyph for 'waters'. Bookending the collection are two sarcophagi. The first is that of King Tut, dead at 19 after being run over by a chariot, whom Howell calls 'my avatar'. When Howell herself was the doomed king's age, her boyfriend 'tried to kill (her) with a Volkswagen'. Since then, she writes, 'I've been resin'd in a vault/of magical thinking, believing I can/spell-cast superstition into art.' When she revisits the image of the sarcophagus, it's now occupied by her dead father, who as he lay dying squeezed her hand so hard that her knuckles bruised, 'as if you'd brawled./As if you'd been the one who buckled him.' Eventually, 'the marks faded/and you ached for those traces.' Her hands are the canvas of a final still life. 'They were proof.'

What makes Howell's debut so resonant is that she's already struck upon art's central paradox. Its impotence is what makes it powerful. Too pure a belief in art is too much like faith, which Howell, in 'A Gospel', attests she lost long ago, and besides, it can't save you:

> My school and church were poverty and violence. A quadriplegic
> classmate lived in a Winnebago. Her mother's ex
> cowered in a laundry hamper with a gun and shot her dead
>   one Sunday after Mass. That's all I know.

In an elegy for a fellow writing student, Howell commiserates with her dead friend over their shared artistic delinquency:

> In retrospect, I marvel
> at what we produced under instruction
> in a microcosm
> that masterfully evaded both love and loss,
> that rugged stuff we are carved out of,
> and break from.

I'm not sure when she wrote that, but if it was during the writing class then there's more than a healthy dose of false modesty in those lines. Notice that even as Howell celebrates breaking free from love and loss, each of those words has the faint umbilicus of a rhyme in the next line, 'loss' clinging to 'stuff', and 'love' clinging to 'out of', that bind-to even as they're breaking-from. There's a kind of Pascal's Wager about Howell's artistic skepticism; poetry may ultimately make nothing happen, but just to hedge your bets you might as well write as if it'll change everything.

And she does. It's a testament to Howell's artistry that even though her debut descends into the darkness of abuse, personal tragedy, mental illness and alcoholism, it never feels begloomed, as it's shot through with the levity and light of her talent. Her ear is impeccable, and she has a gift for mimicry. In 'To the free felons who run your facility', she summons the voice of a paranoid middle-aged man looking for property last seen in 1983. In 'Crunches', she apes some Liberty Village Millennial types, up-speak and all, gearing up for a debauched Halloween: 'I'm going to be a Victoria's Secret angel/which is neat because my name is Victoria?' And then there are the tiny moments of lyric discovery, like these two jingle-ready lines about everyone's preferred NSAID: 'Take an Advil Liqui-Gel;/a little Lake Louise in a pill.' Later, she catches 'A dandelion's geodesic seed-dome scattered.' Watching her father's casket being lowered into the earth, she writes: 'his reliquary swayed over/a salivating hole.' It takes an artist of enormous talent to make even insatiable death sound rapturous.

Howell has a weird syntactic habit. It used to bother me. In prepositional phrases, she drops her possessive pronouns. She writes of 'floral hairpieces/hanging flaccid over ears', the 'our' dropped. About her dead poet friend she notes how he had ' "B E A T"/unironically tattooed on knuckles', omitting 'his'. She does this consistently, and it felt at first like an affectation, the sense being needlessly elided for the sake of concision.

But it turns out that the Egyptian hieroglyph for water, the title of Howell's book, is also a preposition. It doesn't just mean water; it does what water does, flowing into, over, out, on, through. It's remarkably similar to Eliot's theory of the catalytic impersonality of the poet, a philosophy that permeates Howell's stunning debut: that there's an ancient, material, unnamable force that runs through each of us equally, general in its particularity, bookended by coffins our poems can't keep us from.

She writes: 'Anything can happen, and it will./The question is, to whom.' Whatever you call it, this is the work of a gifted poet.

Lazy Bastardism
Carmine Starnino

MICHAEL LISTA: Every Canadian poet has an opinion of Carmine Starnino, and yet his detractors dislike him precisely because he has opinions. When it comes to aesthetics—or at least as they pertain to poetry—Canadians are still Victorians: opinions are fine and all, but they're best kept buried deep within the whalebone corset. Or they're like the Sikh Kirpan, kept sharpened but sheathed, a symbol of the truth's shearing triumph over falsity, only ever drawn if someone else dares disturb the peace and draw his first. And if the time does indeed come for us to start getting stabby, for God's sake do the polite thing—the Canadian thing—and stab me in the back and not in the front, please-and-thank-you, so as to avoid all the awkward eye contact.

Is this the case in the rest of the English-speaking poetry world? Here the poet-critic is at best a tattletale and at worst a scab. They're also, if they dare to write what's pejoratively called 'evaluative criticism', some sort of throwback to a bygone, benighted era when one poem could be better than another. And that's just according to the poets. I have it on good authority, for example, that an earlier, shorter version of one of the pieces in Starnino's most recent book of criticism. *Lazy Bastardism* [2012], on Margaret Atwood, was spiked by one of our daily national newspapers because the appraisal of Atwood (who in Canada is somewhere between a cottage industry and living god-head) was 'negative'.

Starnino is particularly despised by the nebulous consortia we can call the avant-garde; in fact if the avant-garde is a contemporary kind of apophatic theology, disliking Starnino might very well be the *via negativa* that consecrates your membership. The flower of that hatred stems from a single essay, a review from Starnino's more combative first book, of Christian Bök's *Eunoia* (an essay more understood than read) which he deliciously titled, after a Daryl Hine poem published in these pages, 'Vowel Movements'. And his name is sort of a general smear too. After I published a piece of criticism that can broadly be called 'negative', the poet Sina Queyras tweeted that I remind her of Starnino. She meant this as an insult.

What exactly is Starnino as Insult? Everybody knows being a Starnino means being snarky, mean, ad hominem; it means being sesquipedalian, axe-grindy, show-offy; it means being both obstinately contrarian and ostentatiously revisionary, a latter-day Yvor Winters with his provincial road-less-travelled canonizing; it means being close-minded to the new and approbative of the old. But most of all it means one thing—and of all the received, untrue diminishments above, this one is the most contagious, ineluctable and wrong—it means you're 'conservative'.

Conservatism is the worst thing with which a critic can be charged; it implies that you're inured to the only faculty that makes you worth reading—the ability to be surprised by the authentically new and have your mind changed by it. What makes *Lazy Bastardism* so surprising is how seriously it strives for what Starnino himself calls 'unpigeonholeability'. What does Starnino think of visual poetry pioneer bpNichol? Everybody already knows that he would hate him—except he doesn't. He calls Nichol 'too much fun to dislike', and when he faults him, he does so precisely because Nichol wasn't avant-garde enough, writing that, 'Nichol's poetry has fallen short of a crucial threshold: the new that stays news.' What does Starnino think of the poetry of the formally minded Adam Kirsch? Even though everybody already knows that he would love it, he writes that Kirsch's poetry suffers from 'a begloomed, piecemeal rhetoric that feels like padding, and a cookie-cutter form that requires it.'

In other words, the lazy bastard of *Lazy Bastardism* is the -ism itself. And far from being the work of a conservative, I think the book is a challenge to the received liberalism of our time in the same way that Lionel Trilling's *The Liberal Imagination* and Matthew Arnold's 'Culture and Anarchy' were to theirs. The aesthetic opinions at which Starnino inevitably arrives are never preset destinations that have a palpable design upon us, but the good-faith wanderings of a pilgrim with our pleasure in mind, for whom, like Keats, poetry is proved upon the pulse. The book is a raspberry-in-the-face to the lazy leftism that unthinkingly accepts as progressive anything with a vague whiff of syntactic or conceptual transgression; but it also delights in slaughtering the sacred lyric cows whose sanctity we're told to take for granted. These essays are important, I think, not for their conclusions—many of which I disagree with—but for their making public a private canon, a practice that's at the heart of liberalism.

GWYNETH LEWIS: Michael Lista asks if hostility towards evaluative criticism exists in places other than Canada in the English-speaking world. It does. In Britain we seem to be losing the knack for valuing well-argued, considered criticism, let alone dealing constructively with the less well-motivated observations. Ad hominem attacks miss the point, but a passion for the well-being of poetry requires discrimination between the good enough and the best. Poets are, of course, notoriously short on epidermis. Dylan Thomas used to describe the job as walking over broken glass on your eyeballs. I like Starnino's defence of criticism as 'one of the forces that makes poetry possible'. I cheer his attack on that sentimentalization of language which results when you see reading as 'an assertion of integrity rather than an exercise of faculties…. A good poet, in short, will help a reader grow up.'

I agree that it matters less that Starnino is right than the fact that he's grappling with issues that poets need to understand. Sometimes he's silly—he has a rant against the fashion for using epigraphs and states 'style is always happy'. What about style as a defense against pain in Stevie Smith, or Emily Dickinson's 'formal feeling' that's a reaction to suffering? Starnino says, 'There is nothing remotely nurturing or dopamine-inducing about the creative process.' Experiments prove that rhythmic activity in rats produces, er … dopamine. Aside from enjoying the words 'lazy bastardism' in the title, I feel that Starnino never develops it as a tool for judging poetry, though he's bracingly direct about the artistic consequences of vanity, imprecision, and being content with 'faking' a poem.

I had my doubts how much I'd enjoy an account of mainly Canadian poetry without knowing the poems (mea culpa), but this doesn't pretend to be an exhaustive survey so much as what pleases Starnino. I left the book with a list of new enthusiasms: the work of Margaret Avison, Michael Harris, Don McKay, Eric Ormsby, Karen Solie and Peter Trower. I'm not sure I would have ended a volume on my own tradition with a poem of my own, as if it all led up to me. Perhaps Starnino's editor told him it was ok. The big surprise, though, was the similarity between the perceived project of new poetry in Canada and the UK: to 'informalize form—free it from fustiness'. It immediately makes me want to do something else.

ANGE MLINKO: Michael Lista and Gwyneth Lewis concur that the quantity and quality of 'evaluative criticism' is at an all-time low in Canada and Britain respectively. I would add that the same is true in the US. But it's not Victorianism that did it in, here: it's the sense that the lid has been ripped off any consensual definition of poetry, and that for a new generation it has been a test of one's authenticity to write poems that evade all criteria for a 'good poem'. What was once metered speech became *vers libre*, and what was once 'a kind of machine for producing the poetic state of mind' (Valéry), meter or no meter, is now a machine for producing word combinations aimed at one's coterie—or as one says in these parts, 'community'. One need only crack the new edition of the *Norton Anthology of Postmodern Poetry* to see several varieties of this community machine. Such people are fond of pointing out that the word 'poetry' comes from the Greek word *poiesis*, which merely means 'to make'; therefore poetry is essentially nothing more than a 'made thing'.

I blame the genteel evaluative criticism of the eighties and nineties. One got the sense that poetry had become an inbred circle of Lowell/Bishop epigones. Had there been more non–Ivy League, rugged individualists like Carmine Starnino, with similar stature (or notoriety), poetic trends here might not swing so violently between the complacent and the insurrectionary. I don't agree with all his conclusions (I enjoy Medbh McGuckian's private language at its best), but we get pleasure from the same thing in poetry: *sprezzatura*, both in musicality (quoting Eric Ormsby: 'The vacuum's cannistered voracity/never gets enough: its gulf-presidium/snootsavors carpet') and imagism (Robyn Sarah: 'at the back of the palate/the ghost of a rose/in the core of the carrot'). He also admits a bias toward outsiders; as a child of immigrants myself, I too have a distrust of ease. His book's dedication reads: 'In memory of my father … whose choicest words for me when growing up gave this book its title.' To follow suit, I would have to name my collection of criticism, 'I Could Wipe My Heinie with That Piece of Paper' (my MFA). Here's the rub: the wonderful self-skepticism, ambivalence and nuance of Starnino's style has one drawback. The world does not care for skepticism, ambivalence and nuance.

On Poetry
Glyn Maxwell

GL: A tone of ambivalence scarcely appears in Glyn Maxwell's *On Poetry*. He writes in the voice of a teacher on a crusade to persuade his students that writing without form is wrong, wrong, wrong. Maxwell echoes the half-fond, half-contemptuous tone of his teacher Derek Walcott: 'Songwriters stir up a living tradition, poets make flowers grow in air. Bob Dylan and John Keats are at different work. It would be nice never to be asked about this again.' This chutzpah is attractive but it comes at a cost, shutting down speculation so quickly that I was left with distracting 'buts' buzzing inside my head. Maxwell argues that, for songwriters, music plays the role of time that silence does for poets; but doesn't meter—however free—do that for the poet? Doesn't silence surround and inform both art forms?

Maxwell's deity of choice is Time. His beef with free-form poetry is that 'you are effectively saying that time is different these days. It's not what it was. Maybe you think time has been broken.' Quantum physics might be said to have done so, but 'time refracts oddly in the vicinity of verse' is the closest Maxwell comes to a post-Einstein concept of time. He asserts 'poets are voices upon time.' No, *poems* are, there's a big difference. For a poem to live, that voice has to become the reader—and it's on this divide that the terrible fragility of poetry depends.

I've admired Glyn Maxwell's poetry for decades, and there are many fine things in this book. Here's how terza rima behaves: 'This is the creature on the move through life. A new rhyme comes out of the mist, is developed in thought, is left behind.' He discusses Edward Thomas's work as an alternative to T.S. Eliot's high modernism and gives as accurate an account as I know of the impersonal 'I' that arises in a poem:

In unrivalled brimming black, with words you didn't expect, echoes you couldn't foresee, matter you never chose, resonances that crept up around you to wait for your next move. This is not you the writer of poems. This is you the poem, this is you in the language. Not you, you in the language. Not you today, you in time.

Discussing Frost, Maxwell notes 'what looks like repetition isn't repetition.' The book is full of good formalist advice with work-shop ideas, my favourite being pretending that the page is physically hurt or turned on by your every word.

I count myself as being from the same stable as Maxwell, but those buts keep buzzing. He makes an acute point about the sestina as a mainly futile form and proposes it as useless other than for a monologue by a barman serving several customers. Like it or not, the sestina has survived, and therefore, by Maxwell's own criteria, should be poetically viable. In a gesture of typical fluency, Maxwell invents characters for the students in his class and writes poems in each voice.

Maxwell claims that, 'No long-gone poets you can find in books or on websites are long-gone at all: if their pieces survived them they're poets. Work out why they are. Find out what time

knows and you don't.' For my money, time doesn't know anything, and this reading of the poetic canon sounds complacently
ahistorical. Class prejudice, sexism, ageism, religious discrimination all exert force on what may be called poetry and who can
be said to write it. Maxwell is very interesting on the white space
around a poem—for him it represents time. Nevertheless, time
also operates in the black of the words, and at different speeds.
Think of the geology of words, the fingerprints of historical
experience and extra-literary psychological and material pressure, to name a few.

For Maxwell, who writes for the theatre, 'your meeting
with a poem is like your meeting with a person.' Yes ... but
there is an element in language which is non-individual—I
mean political—with and against which the poet has to work. I
keep thinking of Frost's line in 'Home Burial': 'Tell me about it
if it's something human.' Perhaps Rimbaud was more precise
when he said '*Je est un autre*' ('I is another').

Maxwell has strong poetic fathers—we share several—but
he shows little evidence of struggling intellectually with them.
He quotes Joseph Brodsky saying, 'In poetic thought the role of
the subconscious is played by euphony.' This is good, but you
can use the music of a poem to disrupt the natural cadence of the
unconscious—in fact, a poem is a clash between the will and the
unknown. What's missing in this book is the sound of balls
cracking (metaphorically, I mean), the sense of the received
being interrogated and developed in new directions.

The art of poetry exists on a spectrum between versification
and the wider category of poetry. Maxwell confines himself to
verse, the how. The first modern criticism on poetry, Sir Philip
Sidney's *Apology for Poetry* (1595), recognizes that versification
is only half the story: 'One may be a poet without versing, and a
versifier without poetry.' I can't agree that 'the only worthwhile

study the poet, as a *maker*, can make of poetry is—which forms survived and for what reason?' An account of poetry requires attention to 'whatness' as well as 'howness'. The argument between truth and beauty affects the content as well as the form of poetry, and there are legitimate questions to be asked about imagination's morality. Perhaps the book should have been called *On Verse*. Billed as such, this is an original and bravura reiteration of the formalist position. It's of interest as Maxwell's own *ars poetica*, but it has its limitations. 'On Poetry' is yet to be written and requires a wider scope and, maybe, less certainty.

AM: I agree with Gwyneth Lewis: this is a very good book on verse, not 'poetry'. She asks: Is there a book to be written on the *content* of poetry, the 'imagination's morality'? Possibly; but just to stick for a moment with the 'howness' rather than the 'whatness', I was disappointed that Maxwell ducked the most difficult craft question of all, the art of making metaphors: 'that alone cannot be learnt; it is the token of genius. For the right use of metaphor means an eye for resemblances' (Aristotle). Not that Maxwell isn't capable of finding wonderful metaphors himself—his distinction between a poem's 'solar meaning' and 'lunar meaning' will be part of my classroom tool kit forthwith.

To take as an example the lines I quoted from Robyn Sarah, was I really drawn to them because of the versification?

> at the back of the palate
> the ghost of a rose
> in the core of the carrot.

Well, I admit, the anapest-ish bounce of those lines has something to do with their memorability, and the palate/carrot rhyme is indispensable, but the real achievement here is the oxymoronic yoking of the rose and the carrot (smell vs. taste; sweet vs. bitter; pretty vs. nutritive; pink vs. orange). Oxymoronic, but surprisingly *true*—I taste that rose now in raw carrots, indelibly. I think Maxwell would wager that the lightning-strike freshness of metaphor arose organically (no pun intended) from the modulation of the vowels and the fatedness of the rhyme. And there is a lot of truth to the idea that versification is a poetic machinery by which you find yourself saying smarter things than you would have otherwise (to paraphrase James Merrill). But I could just as easily posit that Sarah was actually cutting the top off a carrot, saw the radial symmetry of its core, glimpsed (at a lightning stroke) the visual rhyme with a rose, and constructed the musical lines to be the best container for this metaphor. I'm remembering now Amy Clampitt's glimpse of Perseus's mirrored shield as the progenitor of evolution: 'one wet/eyeblink in the antediluvial dark'. Nature really does advance by mirroring; poets really do have an essential truth at the core of their endeavour when they find resemblances. Maxwell leans on evolutionary biology to bolster his arguments for forms that have 'survived'. He could have taken it further by arguing that these particular forms may have survived, but our job is also to see that metaphors are continually evolving.

ML: I don't think it's just the art of making metaphors that's the difficult question, but the art of making metaphors of form. It takes Maxwell until the final quarter of *On Poetry* to get around to the connection, and when he does it's a bit too freighted for my taste, and a bit too brief: 'Any form in poetry, be it meter, rhyme, line-break, is a metaphor for creaturely life.' Cut the creaturely life bit and you're onto something. Acknowledging the important qualifications Gwyneth Lewis raises as to why some poems survive and some perish, I think what the best poems we've received have in common is that their forms are doing metaphorical work.

To answer Ange Mlinko's question, yes, I do think we're drawn to the Sarah lines in large part because of the versification—it's itself metaphoric. Yes, the 'anapest-ish' bounce is part of it, but so too is the circularity and symmetry of (to use words Maxwell dislikes) the assonance and consonance (at, back, palate/ghost, rose/core, carrot) and that lovely slant rhyme of 'palate' and 'carrot'. The total effect is to give the aural, synesthetic impression of both the cross-cut carrot and the spiralled petals of a rose. The metaphor is itself contained within a mnemonic metaphor, which makes forgetting the lines next to impossible.

Today both bad free verse and bad formalism disappoint for the same reason: the form has been divorced from its metaphor. In the case of bad free verse, the form feels arbitrarily default, like a font. With bad formalism, it feels willfully decorative, like a font. When poems of each kind succeed, it's because their containers—poetry is the only art form that is its own container—are constructed out of the materials of their contents, in a kind of infinite feedback loop. No one has done this better than Dante. When Maxwell writes about *The Comedy*'s terza rima he never looks beyond the lineation of the canto. But each of the three canticles is made up of thirty-three cantos, and so the whole three-book poem is shaped by the fractal Thomism of the triune God. Form achieves a cosmological meaning; hell, purgatory and heaven are governed by the same ineluctable laws. The three great American free-versifiers—Whitman, Eliot, and Ashbery—succeed because they each achieve a distinct formal meaning: Whitman's is the expansiveness of the manifest destiny of self; Eliot's is the failing and fragmentation of the old Western order; Ashbery's, the channel-surfing ticker of thought.

Taking this too far leads to what Yvor Winters called the fallacy of imitative form (and for my money lots of George Herbert's concrete poems in *The Temple* jumped the shark before Canadians and Brazilians made a movement out of them hundreds of years later). But I have to agree with Maxwell that some of the freshest poetry today is employing some of the stalest techniques, because the techniques are taking on new meanings that free verse can't accommodate: the intractability of human nature in A.E. Stallings, the tautologies of late capitalism in Michael Robbins, the equivalent pleasures of high and low culture in David McGimpsey.

Madness, Rack, and Honey
Mary Ruefle

AM: Mary Ruefle shares Glyn Maxwell's preoccupation with time and poetry, but her method and conclusions could not be more different. They both begin at the beginning, yet even their beginnings diverge. Maxwell puts us on the savannah with Pleistocene man (and, implicitly, Denis Dutton, whose best-selling *The Art Instinct: Beauty, Pleasure, and Human Evolution* popularized the view that our conventional notions of beauty are an evolutionary adaptation). Ruefle's first essay, 'On Beginnings', places us somewhere in the vicinity of Genesis, Paul Valéry, and the pre-Socratics. That is, her first sentence would not sound out of place in a collection of Heraclitean or Pythagorean aphorisms: 'In life, the number of beginnings is exactly equal to the number of endings: no one has yet to begin a life who will not end it.' As for Valéry: 'the opening line of a poem, he said, is like finding a fruit on the ground, a piece of fallen fruit you have never seen before, and the poet's task is to create the tree from which such a fruit would fall.' Next to this Symbolist tree of knowledge Ruefle sets 'In the beginning was the Word'—and thus puts us in a terrain closer to metaphysics than evolutionary psychology.

There didn't seem to be room in Maxwell's short, pithy and *urgent* book for an acknowledgement like Ruefle's:

The only purpose of this lecture, this *letter*, my only intent, goal, object, desire, is to waste time. For there is so little time to waste during a life, what little there is being so precious, that we must waste it, in whatever way we come to waste it, with all our heart.

And unlike Maxwell (but more like Starnino), Ruefle embraces her own oscillations in mood and opinion over time. She often recalls her younger self and notes the changes of mind that mark a decades-long obsession with poetry: 'When I look back at [*A Vision*] now and read some of the passages my nineteen-year-old hand underlined, I sometimes laugh out loud.' Maybe this is why her essay 'Poetry and the Moon' is so wise. In English poetry, the fickle mistress changes like the moon; as do the arts, which in Raleigh's words, 'vary by esteeming'. Does this make poetry an insubstantial thing? Far from it. Ruefle notes the intersection of the literal-historical (NASA's moon) and the poetical (Yeats's moon, or Sappho's). Rather than obsolescing the poetical, the literal—as with all solid bodies—is simply folded into the poetical as a form of memory. Time, we see, turns everything into poetry. Fact.

The expansive Ruefle doesn't argue so much as she meanders, digresses, and juxtaposes; her awareness that she is helping us *waste our time* compels her to be as charming and humorous and equanimous as a good host. Yet she is not giving us anything so concrete as a set of tools with which to write poetry. And I do mean poetry, not verse. Her titles seem to promise information—'On Beginnings', 'Poetry and the Moon', 'On Sentimentality', 'On Secrets'. But she is likely to say, as she does of metaphor, that poetry 'doesn't actually exist, insofar as it does not reside in nature, but it exists insofar as it spontaneously arises in the human mind as a perceptual event. To conceive of things that don't exist is a *natural* act for a human being.'

Her 'Short Lecture on Craft' seems to poke fun at the whole notion; it takes the form of a pun: 'By 700 bc the Phoenicians were sailing.' That is, 'craft' is a boat, and moreover, 'the most primitive craft is a raft, whose very word is embedded in the word *craft*.' While she paints a picture of unknown Polynesian raft-builders (much as Maxwell paints us a picture of the savannah dwellers), she points us toward another dictionary definition of craft: 'skill in evasion or deception'. 'Those unknown men and women lashing together their gigantic raft, what were they evading, whom were they deceiving? Were they evading hunger, disaster, unspeakable loss?' Ruefle ends her parable with apophatic rapture: 'But surely there must have been a moment of glorious well-being when they slid their raft into the water and discovered that it could float, and would hold them all, as they set out to cut a hole in time.'

Notice how poems *cut a hole* in time rather than *master* time, as Maxwell claims measure does. Which do we want: to manipulate time or to confuse it? To make it stand still or to escape it—carried off, as the etymology of 'rapture' would have it, in a divine kidnapping?

ML: '*Apophatic* rapture'—yes, and there's that word again. Part of what makes this one of the most moving books on poetry in recent memory is how infrequently it's actually *about* poetry. But of course it's never about anything else. That's the genius of Ruefle's dialectic: she can always have it both ways. 'True or false; the subject or topic of a poem is never really its subject or topic.' Notice that isn't a question, but here's one: How should one write about theme in poetry? By writing about Polartec Fleece bathrobes, Shaker and Las Vegas civic design, the Walt Disney Florida town of Celebration—everything except theme in poetry, of course. 'The two sides of a secret are repression and expression, just as the two sides of the poem are the told and untold.' Or as Aristotle said, by way of Auden: the mark of genius is being able to hold two incongruous thoughts in one's head at once.

As Ange Mlinko observes, Ruefle's circular way of thinking comes from her marrying the twin chambers of Western poetry—the Hebraic and the Hellenic. The result is cardiovascular thinking, the arterial going-forth of Genesis-Exodus, and the venous return of the Odyssey. The best example of this is in her essay 'On Sentimentality'. First, in her understated fashion, she coaxes us into understanding early Modernism (or Imagism) in a new way:

The effect of an image in a poem often acts like a kitten: we are expected to go '*ah*' deep down in our interior sphere, and to slightly elevate ourselves in relation to the world, as if the soul were a beach ball.

Purring, big-eyed, and there—*Of course* an image is sentimental; in a poem an image is only just barely words, so undeservedly convincing of a feeling it can't even bring itself to express! But what is sentimentality? A 'causeless emotion'. Then Ruefle writes: 'one day I realized that *causeless emotion* was an even better definition of *poetry*.'

So whereas Starnino and Maxwell focus on verse, which is made of words, how the mechanics of words in a poem please and disappoint, Ruefle is focused on poetry, the Word, which isn't just pre-material, but pre-linguistic. Isn't every poem the record of its failed reckoning with the impulse that inspired it? How then can we possibly write about that shadow-side of poetry, its perfect pre-verbal dimension, which even in the best poems we can only get glimpses of? Apophatically. *Madness, Rack, and Honey* does just that: 'The poem, once begun, is so physical that it cannot realize itself: like an actual physical event (not like a poem at all) it must die, finish, or end *without completion*.' Which seems to suggest, thankfully, that whatever hunger makes us love poetry can't be satisfied by poems alone.

GL: Michael Lista asks how it's possible to write about the pre-verbal dimension of poetry. Indirectly, it's the ur-subject for poets—Coleridge's pleasure-dome, Dante's paradise. But it's mainly the way each poet's mind sashays to the subconscious wordless tune whose rhythmical impulses dictate all form. (The best account I know of this is in theologian Jacques Maritain's Mellon lectures, *Creative Intuition in Art and Poetry*.) Michael Lista's formulation of poetry as a 'mnemonic metaphor' is exactly right.

Mary Ruefle's book is the fruit of fifteen years' lecturing and it shows. She explores the poetic hinterland of the human mind. Ruefle's insight about the skies took my breath away: 'Stars were the first *text*, the first instance of gabbiness; connecting the stars, making a pattern out of them, was the first *story*, sacred to storytellers.' There is a theory that the *Iliad*'s epic images were originally devised to recall the movement of the stars.

Ruefle makes a powerful case for the irreality (her word) of poetry: 'I love pretension. It is a mark of human earthly abstraction, whereas humility is a mark of human divine abstraction. I will have all of eternity in which to be humble, while I have but a few short years to be pretentious.' I'd answer that humility gets you a piece of heaven ahead of schedule. I'm not as sure as Ange Mlinko that time 'turns everything into poetry', it tends to dust around here. At times, Ruefle's book becomes a compendium of quotes, but I found new gems.

I'm intrigued by a point that both Ruefle and Maxwell raise, that 'images and metaphors are often rhetorical stand-ins.' For what? As she mentions René Girard's work, I wondered if she was about to argue for poem as scapegoat. The French theologian depicts Christ as the place onto which we project all that we most hate and fear, though we know him to represent the truth. If poetry's a similar scapegoat, then that would explain our ambivalent feelings towards it.

This book is useful about other aspects of being a poet: 'I want to say the poet is never afraid because he is unceasingly afraid … you might say fear *is* the poet's procedure, that which he has been trained to concentrate on.' Thank God for a poet who values silence as much as talking: 'I used to think I wrote because there was something I wanted to say.... But I know now I continue to write because I have not yet heard what I have been listening to.'

JAN ZWICKY

In 2012, the Canadian Women in the Literary Arts (CWILA) foundation launched with the mandate to analyze and ultimately reverse the gender imbalance in book reviewing in Canada. The organization, founded by Gillian Jerome, analyzed the book reviews published last year by literary journals, general-interest magazines and newspapers, and tallied both the gender of the authors under review and the gender of the reviewers. As a country, we fared better than our American counterparts (as scored by VIDA, the U.S. equivalent to CWILA), but not by much. I'd recommend every reader of this column go to the website, take in the analysis, read the interviews and essays, and think the issue over, because it's an important one, and the work that was put into the study is as impressive as the results are humbling.

One of the many threads in the broader discussion is a call for women to do more reviewing. I second it, and I imagine that CWILA will inspire women who hadn't reviewed before now to start. And yet on the eve of what many hope is a new era of criticism in Canada, I was surprised to find that one of the three essays framing the CWILA discussion is one by Jan Zwicky entitled 'The Ethics of the Negative Review', which we can charitably call spooky and meretricious, but is probably deserving of a much less friendly repudiation. The essay justifies her baffling policy of not publishing negative reviews during her tenure in the 1990s as review editor of *The Fiddlehead*, a major Canadian literary journal. 'I made a point,' she writes, 'of requesting that a review be written only if the reviewer was genuinely enthusiastic about the book.' Why? Because to be an artist, 'one must be tuned to the play of emotion and perception' and therefore reviewers should have 'respect for the thin skin that is essential to creativity.'

Cue the violins, folks. The essay, woozy with Romantic anemia, begins by paraphrasing Byron's idiotic diagnosis that 'the critics killed Keats' (Keats died of an infection of the tubercle bacillus, TB), and along its way manages to summon every black-beret cliché about the poetic temperament, so that by its conclusion we can all but smell Chatterton's extinguished candle. And beneath those black berets are the empty heads of red herrings and straw men. The idea that a poet's power is in any way related to his predisposition to take offence is stupid beyond stupid; if it were true, Shakespeare, the most linguistically and emotionally perceptive poet in the language, would have folded up tent in 1592, well before he reached the height of his powers, when Richard Greene published his scathing review of 'the upstart Crowe' who 'supposes he is as well able to bombast out a blanke verse as the best.' How, Jan, did he ever go on?

I feel a little bashful pointing out to a professional philosopher that she's constructing a false syllogism, but Zwicky does just that when she proposes that only a positive appraisal is 'engaged with its subject matter'. Anyone who has read a scathing review by Randall Jarrell or Helen Vendler or William Logan can tell you that critic and subject matter are not just engaged, but betrothed. They're flat-out honeymooning. 'I've seen too many beginning poets discover Donne,' she contends, to believe that criticism needs to jolt our preconceptions, because a classic's greatness 'lies precisely in its ongoing ability to move, provoke and inspire an audience.' But if it weren't for T. S. Eliot's punchy essay 'The Metaphysical Poets', Donne, who every fledgling poet now considers indispensable, would still be as neglected as he was for centuries, when everyone knew he was beyond derivative. And am I the only one who finds Zwicky's assertion hilarious that 'historically, Virginia Woolf provides us with some excellent models' of cheerful, uncontroversial criticism? The author of *A Room of One's Own*, no slouch in either the artistic or critical (not to mention feminist) departments, wrote: 'my real delight in reviewing is to say nasty things.'

So what's Zwicky's advice to the women who, inspired by CWILA to change the critical landscape, find themselves in the not-uncommon position of being assigned to review a book which they dislike? 'I am suggesting simply that, in public, we keep our mouths shut.' What a miserable, low thing to tell another woman, another writer, another human. No, it's more than that: It's unethical. I'm sorry, but we've tried it Zwicky's way: flat, uninspired review prose that reads like it was composed by publicists playing duelling games of mad libs and broken telephone; swollen reputations left to inflate and float away; living under the general paranoia that simply speaking your mind is enough to ruin your future prospects.

Enough. Look: love is Janus-faced. Being turned by a work of art reorients your whole perspective, the part that loves and the part that hates, and there's nothing wrong with admitting that certain word-orders now move you more than others. Call me old-fashioned, but I think the truth sounds beautiful, and there's an intrinsic value in discovering what writers think of each other's work. The purpose of a review, good or bad, is to begin a conversation, not to end it. And when we write a negative review, we're writing it about an adult, a professional, who of her own volition chose to publish poems, to share them with other human beings who have that pesky, intractable habit of thinking for themselves. No one is forcing these people, we who are too many, to publish; if you're squeamish, put your poems in a goddamn drawer. And if you can't stomach the occasional reader disclosing that she doesn't like your poems, well: There's always law school.

POSTSCRIPT: My essay on Jan Zwicky stirred up a lot of silt when it was first published. Everyone in the Canadian literary scene seemed to weigh in on it, including Zwicky herself, who asked to publish a rebuttal in the pages of the *Post*. In it, she called me incompetent, illiterate, and said that I should be fired. Zwicky's partisans rejoiced. Here's how I responded:

1. If you find yourself enjoying this exchange, keep in mind that what Zwicky has written is a negative review of another writer's work, unconscionable to write and unethical to publish. If you think her most recent argument is persuasive in content, remember that its form is all the while conspiring against it.

2. I was tough on Zwicky's arguments, but I reserved my criticism for the writing, and not the writer. I call her essay 'spooky' and her idea that a writer's power is generated by his ability to take offence 'stupid'. Zwicky, however, calls me illiterate and incompetent, and even goes so far as to insinuate that I be estranged from one of the means of my livelihood. You don't need to follow Zwicky down the *ad hominem* path if you want to be, on occasion, a 'negative reviewer'. But that's exactly what she wants you to think. Zwicky doesn't distinguish between censuring the art and censoring the artist, because the former is an almost corporeal extension of the latter. Worse, Zwicky's logic doesn't distinguish between saying someone's argument is wrong and then suggesting that he should join the ranks of the unemployed. Which is doubly dangerous—it eventually makes libel of criticism, and criticism of libel.

3. I'm not surprised by the number of writers who applaud

Zwicky's argument that professional critics should keep their mouths shut in public. To those of you, I still advise: be careful. Despite Zwicky's erudition and accomplishments, she's offering you a poisoned chalice. Following Twitter yesterday, it looked like the argument is mostly fracturing along camp and gender lines, which is disappointing. I'll freely admit that people may take exception with the fact that I am the one making this argument, and may even make the mistake of assuming that this argument somehow emanates out of the prejudice some people have accused me of. Some of you may take pleasure in my undressing even at the expense of the argument that franchises it. People can dislike me, and dislike the way I review, but in my experience the character of a writer doesn't discredit the validity of her arguments. In other words, the real purchase of the argument exists beyond its advocates. This is about a critic's moral right to full and free expression.

4. Refining her bit about Socrates: Wasn't he sentenced to death for corrupting the minds of the youth into questioning the gods of the state?

5. In lots of ways I can't win this argument, as uncontroversial as its central premise may be. The people who have the most to gain from listening to it are also the ones who have the most to lose by my being right. But nothing can shake my conviction that a literary culture is healthier, wealthier and more worthy of being passed down to the generation behind us, when we're not smilingly bullied into abandoning its free inquiry. But we'll see. My friend Jason Guriel (whose own defence of negative criticism in *Poetry Magazine* is worth a read or re-read) wrote me yesterday: 'Canada gets the poetry culture it deserves.'

ALEXANDRA OLIVER

This is Alexandra Oliver's 'Over a Fabergé Owl':

> A bright-eyed but humourless thing
> stands vigil, as the day grows dark,
> its plume a shield, cold as a shield.
> Its gaze ignores the view, the park.
> Fussed over for its wild worth,
> itemized in estimates and wills,
> it disregards all human ills,
> while the inheritors of Earth
> (unmarbled, with no Tsarist sheens),
> outside, as roughened moonlight blanches,
> wait: wrath keen in the evergreens,
> claws calmly gripping those live branches.

After reading that, here's the last thing you think: a slam poet
wrote that. Weirdly, it's also true. A slam poet wrote that. Like
Keats's eternal Grecian urn, which will 'remain, in midst of
other woe/than ours', when 'old age shall this generation
waste', Oliver's Fabergé Owl 'disregards all human ills' while
wrath 'claws calmly gripping those live branches'. And also
like Keats, Oliver is describing her own art by way of an arti-
fact: well-wrought, filigree, gleaming, a human vessel made
cold and hard to withstand time's depredations. It's an unchar-
acteristically permanent sentiment for a slam poet (or any of
the Goldsmithian post-poetry poets waiting to inherit the
Earth).

But Oliver's transformation from a '90s slam scene

mainstay into a bricks-and-mortar formalist is as misleading as it is unlikely. You can find some of Oliver's old performances on YouTube, including her appearance in the documentary *Slam Nation* from almost 20 years ago; what's clear is that Oliver was never quite a slam poet. Here is the opening of one of her poems from *Slam Nation*:

> Hello my name is Mary Lou,
> Your phone sex partner for tonight.
> I'm five-foot-four, blue-eyed and white.
> My legs are fat. My chest is flat.
> And though my teeth are fairly bright,
> I have horrendous over-bite.

The elements that make an Oliver poem so distinct are here: the cinematic tableaux, the Dr Seuss After Dark diction (here Cindy Lou is a very grown up Mary Lou), and even the masterfully unsubtle meter that Oliver later employed (with much more sophistication) in 'Over a Fabergé Owl', iambic tetrameter. What's notable about Oliver's presence on the slam scene is how unlike her contemporaries she was. She eschewed the hip-hop-inspired verse paragraphs of densely assonant phrasing used by everyone from Saul Williams to Shane Koyczan, and instead delivered, in her trademark flat affect and drill sergeant's bark, her twisted nursery rhymes as if Lynn Crosbie had dressed up as Yeats for Remembrance Day.

Twenty years on, Biblioasis has released Oliver's Canadian debut, *Meeting the Tormentors in Safeway*, one of the funniest, most deeply felt, and formally ingenious collections in recent memory. Oliver, who also holds a degree in film studies, writes poems that have dual purchase on the senses; she is equally gifted at picture-perfect scene making and image construction as she is at stitching those scenes together in an unforgettable aural fabric. In 'A Child's Christmas in the Socialist Federal Republic of Yugoslavia', Oliver recalls an episode from her childhood, when someone else's mother, 'a nimbus of perfume', singled her out to address a drunken Santa Claus in some miserable church basement in a doomed country. She writes:

> I peered into the brandy-bleary stare
> and burbled out the fragments of a speech
> that scattered like a country blown apart.

The book's title poem recalls a schoolyard bully with:

> that laugh, which sounds like a hundred birds
> escaping from a gunshot through the reeds.

Technically, nothing seems out of Oliver's grasp. Her go-to iambic pentameter can swallow anything in its path. The mysterious life of a European symphony conductor is captured in the deceptively meticulous music of her terza rima. 'Doug Hill' sees Oliver inventing a new form, something between terza rima and a villanelle, to do justice to the obsessive histrionics of young love. In 'The Gulls', Oliver transforms the sonic impact of rhyme and meter into an abusive partner's assault:

> My smiling, pale son goes off to play.
> A truck is parked beside the ice cream shack
> and, from a falcon's wing, big knuckles crack
> against a woman's jaw. I hear him say,
> You keep your smart mouth shut. I take the fries,
> try not to watch the bruised flight of her back.
> The gulls beg off now, swallowed in soft cries.

Meeting the Tormentors in Safeway should go a long way toward establishing Oliver as one of the country's best stanza makers, with a fluidity and ambition aspiring to Dylan Thomas or Yeats. A trademark Oliver stanza is an eight- or ten-liner, where the first line rhymes with the last, the second with the second last, and so on, with a couplet in the middle. The form achieves a philosophical effect that dovetails with the book's title; that the snares and eventualities of human destiny, what Oliver calls 'The Enigma of Fate', are predicated on the randomness and headlong freedom of youth.

Not every poem succeeds. Poems that rely too heavily on the list, the catalogue and anaphora are almost always boring. But the way they fail is instructive; however uninspired the routine, Oliver always sticks a landing. Her work was forged in performance, and she seems to have internalized something that Larkin, reviewing Betjeman, wrote: 'A direct relation with the reading public could be established by anyone prepared to be moving and memorable.' When she fails, she fails entertainingly. When she succeeds, she succeeds entirely. And I'll bet it's Oliver's maturation in the slam scene that made her conscious of the pitfalls and possibilities of a breathing audience before her, by whose enjoyment her poems live or die.

RICARDO STERNBERG

The most famous retirement in literature is a magician's. *The Tempest*'s final act is an extended swan song not just for Prospero, but for the sorcerer who conjured him. When I first encountered the name Ricardo Sternberg, it was in the pages of Carmine Starnino's collection of essays *A Lover's Quarrel*, and it was evident that some of Prospero's rough magic was at work on the critic, a man who to many in the world of Canadian letters is something of a Caliban. At the time, Starnino, bored of the lexically inert inheritors of Al Purdy, went in for more conspicuously explosive language. But Sternberg's poems remind me less of pyrotechnics than smoldering coals—which as it turns out is where the real heat is anyways. His poems are peopled by mermaids and angels, are visited by daemons and devils, and journey enchanted seas to imaginary islands. In other words, they charm.

Magic, by definition, is an exemption to the natural order, and the first thing readers notice and admire about Sternberg's poems is the overwhelming sense that they shouldn't work as well as they do. Their constituent parts are too simple; the language is that of everyday speech, sparingly multi-syllabic and rarely sending you to the dictionary. Faulkner once said something like that to Hemingway and intended it as an insult. But Hemingway knew that it's hard to cast a spell on someone whose nose is in the OED. And that's just it: Sternberg's poems operate the same way that spells do. He describes his own technique as 'slowly blowing breath/into each syllable', and even here we can see the magic at work: the expertly weighted lines balanced by alternating alliteration, the bookending L sounds, the enjambment machine-tooled to correspond to the length of a breath.

But what puts the lines over is that the mechanics of the artistry are hidden in the rafters, leaving only the illusion onstage. The sense is less that the magic has been muscled into place than that Sternberg has divined the secret connections between words, unlocking their hypnotic qualities. As Quintilian said, 'the perfection of art is to conceal art.' It leaves us feeling that the laws of nature have been upended, like seeing the magician's coin vanish from his hands and, abracadabra, appearing behind your ear.

We ask Sternberg the question we ask the magician: How did you do it? One of his tricks draws on Frost's definition of good poetry: 'Like a piece of ice on a hot stove, the poem must ride on its own melting.' What does that mean? Like a spell (think of the spells of the witches of *Macbeth*, for example), the poem must be self-contained, self-actualizing and self-consuming, enacting the recipe it mnemonically encodes, and using only its own materials for transportation. A perfect example is these lines of Sternberg's, about a group of sailors lost at sea: 'We sailed as we could:/now for the sake of sailing/the silk sheen of the sea,/its blue susurrus.' Listen to how the lines treadle themselves up and down as a ship does over a swell. And like its sailors venturing into the unknown without a map, the alliterative 's' sounds build toward the perfectly placed 'susurrus', a word that not only means, but sonically re-creates, the inhuman babble of the open ocean. Like the entropic piece of ice, or a spell, the sense of the poem consumes itself at exactly the moment its power is fully realized.

In his review of Sternberg's masterpiece of a second book, *Map of Dreams*, Starnino characterizes the incantatory qualities of Sternberg's verse as being consistent with prayer. This, I think, is untrue. Prayers, though they may share an origin with spells, operate in a fundamentally different way. Whereas spells are seductive, prayers are ingratiating; whereas spells are charming, prayers are obsequious. If a spell works, it's only because its craftsmanship and delivery were unimpeachable. Spells have a materiality, an efficacy, an accountability that prayers lack, what Sternberg himself calls his 'algebraic incantations'.

Most important of all though is that while the object of a prayer is an inscrutable god, whose reaction we can't gauge, the object of a spell is the physical world, and often a human being. The magician, then, unlike the supplicant, can't ever take his audience for granted. And unlike the petitioner, the magician knows when he's failed. One of my favourite Sternberg poems, 'The Alchemist', from his debut *The Invention of Honey*, homes directly in on poetry as magic:

> You will find
> the laboratory
> far simpler these days;
> uncluttered.
> The cauldron is gone,
> the endless bubbling,
> the stench, the maze
> of pipes, the shelves
> of exotic ingredients
> that, however combined,
> could not transmute
> baseness into gold.
> That is all done with.
> Sold or given away
> to whoever would have it.

The thin blue flame
went out.

But I have abandoned
more than tools.
The obstinate ideas
have been driven out
and I am now plagued
by something different
whose needs are simpler:
pen and paper and time
to apply one to the other.
There is no conjuring
but that which a pen
might drum
across the surface;
there is no incantation
but that which language
performs upon itself:
word linking with magic
word, the whole sustained
by the musculature of syntax.

Mystery is what remains
constant; mystery of magic
and of failure:
my nightmare of metal
forever dull,
replaced by this page
that remains blank
though I write upon it.

As far as I'm concerned, you can't consider that poem a failure. But then why does the mystery of poetry remain constant? Why does Sternberg write, cryptically, that the page 'remains blank/though I write upon it'? Is the blank page the part of it that remains unwritten upon? No. The page remains blank even when it's black with ink, because the true surface of the poem isn't the page; it's the person who's reading it. Like a spell, the poem is inert until it's cast on its intended target: you.

Like any magician worth his salt, Sternberg can conjure from thin air. In his poem 'Onions', he's got voodoo for your Vidalia, writing: 'The opacity of onions/is deceiving.//The onion is a crystal ball/that makes you cry/for future sorrows.' In 'Buffalo', Sternberg is cheeky about his conjuring, writing, 'I have wrestled a buffalo/into this poem/the least I could do/for an endangered species.' And then, in a trick straight out of *Inception*, he writes, 'the reader is to blame/who brings red into this poem.'

But as everyone from David Copperfield to David Blaine knows, the crowds come for the disappearing acts. Like any top-hatted illusionist, Sternberg starts with birds. In 'Oriole Weather', he wonders if orioles fly the skies over his home. Later he writes, 'But oriole, the word,/flutters around me now/as it has all week/unaddressed/until at last I write//south//and it goes.' Poof.

But zooming out, and surveying Sternberg's oeuvre as a whole, we can see that a grander, more fundamental disappearing act has been taking place beneath our noses. Beginning with his third book, *Bamboo Church*, magic itself, as a subject, was being transformed. In his first two books, *The Invention of Honey*, and *Map of Dreams*, the fantastical, by occupying the foreground of the poem, remained hypothetical. An early poem in *Bamboo Church* alerts us to the fact that by submerging magic in its particulars, he's made it general. Here's 'Quark':

Consider the quark: its existence
is posited by scientists entranced
by a nothing which is there;
a particle that does not share
the known properties of materiality:
there but not there: a ghost entity.

Cyril of Thessalonika argued the case:
God withdrew and thus freed space
for the expanding universe. Absence
was his gift which makes his presence
this oxymoron worthy of contemplation:
the Zero at the core of all creation.

Like Coleridge attending scientific lectures to replenish his stock of metaphors, by hitting the books, the purview of Sternberg's sorcery has penetrated the natural world more deeply than ever before. And buried here in the irony of quantum mechanics—that at the centre of everything is nothing—is an even deeper irony: by becoming more secular, the god withdrawn, Sternberg's poems became even more magical.

His best trick he saves for last: love. When a magician aims his gifts at our hearts, we call the voodoo charisma. I'm spelling it out here because as you may have noticed, Canadian writers are notoriously short on charisma, and maybe as a result, are famously unsuccessful as lovers. It's not pretty; if someone isn't getting a hook in the eye, then they're staring a little too long and immodestly at a bear. Sternberg, unlike the rest of us, has moves. To my mind, he's the best living poet of love in our country. Bookending his oeuvre are dances. His first book's first poem, 'The True Story of My Life', is the dramatic monologue of a young prince being groomed for an arranged, aristocratic marriage. After lessons in 'personal magnetism,' and dancing—most notably 'the courtship dance'—the prince absconds with, and elopes, a commoner. In the final, title poem of his most recent book, 'Some Dance', we find the prince and his bride again, the poet and his wife, as they wash the dishes and dance in their kitchen. Across the distance between these two poems, we can trace Sternberg's imaginative journey, from the mythical, enchanted beginnings to the secular magic of dancing in a darkened kitchen. Even there, the conjurer can wring a spell out of a hand towel: 'You wash and rinse. / I dry and stack.'

How does Sternberg do it? Here's a thought. Magic, like love, and like poetry, is a contract. We furnish the conjurer, the poet, and the lover, with the raw material of our imagination, which is their stage. We supply the lock in which their key is turned. Sternberg can transport us because he can look into us, deeper than did ever plummet sound, and see the imaginary islands to which we dream to travel—in poetry, in magic, and in love. The world conspires against all three. Today may begin his retirement, but in Ricardo Sternberg is a Prospero whose staff won't break, whose books won't drown.

DON McKAY

'To write,' quipped Don McKay in *Birding, or desire*, the book that made him famous, requires 'an elementary understanding of the place of human psychology/among nature's interlocking food chains.' That same nose for sociobiology will come in handy in trying to understand how McKay became, according to the publisher of his Collected Poems and just about everybody else in our food chain, the 'pre-eminent Canadian poet'.

After the false starts of *Long Sault*'s rambling Purdyisms and the Ted Hughes–inspired persona myth of *Lependu*, the McKay we know today emerged in 1983's *Birding, or desire*. So much of what Canadian poetry became in the intervening decades has its origins there: a street-wise, rapid-fire vernacular, intertextuality (*The Birds of Canada* ever within reach), environmentalism, Bach. 'Close-Up on a Sharp-Shinned Hawk', which has aged better than much of the collection, is McKay at his best—and worst:

> Concentrate upon her attributes:
> the accipiter's short
> roundish wings, streaked breast, talons fine
> and slender as the X-ray of a baby's hand.
> The eyes (yellow in this hatchling
> later deepening to orange then
> blood red) can spot
> a sparrow at four hundred meters and impose
> silence like an overwhelming noise
> to which you must not listen.

Suddenly, if you're not careful, everything
goes celluloid and slow
and threatens to burn through and you
must focus quickly on the simple metal band around her leg
by which she's married to our need to know.

McKay often starts poems the way my dad used to spoil car trips: by telling you what to pay attention to. The hawk we're concentrating on goes by an exotic technical name—a trick poets would pick up from McKay—'accipiter'. We get all sorts of hermeneutic data about the hawk, another of McKay's heritable traits. The poem's own 'short, roundish wings' are formally expressed in the blank verse of its opening and closing lines. And McKay deserves kudos for wrangling 'X-ray' into a poem, maybe a first for Canadian poetry. The X-ray simile of the talons as baby bones, both violent and delicate, is the high-water mark of the piece, and yet it's a rare gesture for McKay, who's spent a lifetime avoiding seeing the human in the natural world. The last three lines of the first stanza have all the grace of a plane crash, leaning heavily on sonorous but exhausted poeticisms. Junk too is everything until the last two lines of the poem, which are key to understanding McKay's oeuvre. The lines sound great, the falconer's shackle a kind of epistemological wedding band, but constitute dubious poetic thinking. Just as the band is an imposition on the natural sovereignty of the hawk, so too is thinking about her in human—or poetic—terms. Standing in opposition to the best moment in the poem, the X-ray simile when the human is seen in the natural, it's a beautifully written excuse to get out of the business of poetry.

Here is McKay's collected works, the horrendously titled *Angular Unconformity*, writ small. Truth is: it's a mixed bag, and has been for half a century. Even as McKay has been transforming into one of the forces of nature that loom over his poems, it's hard not to think that he may have anticipated us getting him wrong. Like the other eco-minded poets of his generation—especially Tim Lilburn—McKay hasn't placed much faith in human intelligence. He only anthropomorphizes the thanatonic. In lines that anticipate the best of early Anne Carson, McKay writes: 'Sleep,/off somewhere tinkering with his motorcycle' and 'Death is outside in his pickup truck'. At the end of *Birding, or desire* he writes: 'The brain roots for its words, essentially/a pig. Not quite smart enough/to not get fat.' In rooting (in both senses) for the often empty calories of McKay's words, our waistlines lengthening and blood sugar spiking, too many of us have succumbed to our national disease: McKayabetes.

The question is: Why McKay? Why did he, and not the half-dozen or so other top poets of his generation (who I suppose are now post-eminent), become the institution? There are a couple of reasons. By the time *Birding, or desire* appeared in 1983, McKay, with his ear for vernacular and rural affectations, looked like a natural inheritor of Purdy's laureateship—itself rather dubious, looking back. His ecological high-mindedness was glossed with just enough aesthetic disaffection to make him seem cool, an attribute, real or imagined, about which Canadian poets are hysterically self-conscious. And the drive of his poems, all torque and no traction, dovetailed nicely with the emerging poetics of trying to get nowhere as quickly as possible (which itself is a cliché: 'it's less about the destination than the journey').

But that doesn't explain it. McKay, as the jacket copy of *Angular Unconformities* stresses, made his living as a teacher, mentor, editor and publisher to an entire generation of Canadian poets. He taught at the University of Western Ontario and the University of New Brunswick. At the Banff Centre for the Arts, he mentored a young Karen Solie and Ken Babstock, members of the middle generation of Canadian poets at work today, which feels McKay's influence most acutely. Babstock thanks McKay in *Mean*'s acknowledgements as 'UncleLear', positioning himself as the Fool to McKay's mad king, but McKay could bequeath his kingdom to a generation of Canadian poets, and still keep his knights. In Canadian poetry's tight-knit serfdom, the paucity of dissenting reviews about McKay's work has everything to do with the fact that McKay, by all accounts, is beloved as a man. Amiability, rather than acumen, is our acme.

It has to be said: if you put McKay cheek-to-jowl with other top, but less socially influential, practitioners of his generation, his work pales. Let's meet him on his home turf, nature writing. Here he is on flora: 'Flowers begin inhaling through their roots/exhaling darkness.' Again, McKay goes in for the sonorous vagary. Here's the ex-pat Eric Ormsby on another flora, lichens: 'Far-off they're starlike, spiky as galaxies./Like us they clutch and grip their chilly homes/And the wind defines their possibilities.' Not only is he more magisterial by being precise, Ormsby doesn't so much anthropomorphize the lichens as floralize us, and in doing so sees the natural world in the human X-ray. Here's the exquisite Robyn Sarah on a desiccated bouquet: 'Brittle, dry and brown,/it seemed to speak too plainly of a waste/of friendship, forced to flower, culled in haste.'

It's hard not to think of McKay when reading Sarah's lines, and of a career 'forced to flower' beyond the true merit of his poems. If you doubt that the ubiquity of McKay's influence, and the uniformity of his praise, is the result of his personal, not literary, appeal, then just imagine if it had been Eric Ormsby—or Robyn Sarah, or Bruce Taylor—editing and mentoring those

taste makers. It wasn't a sinister plot or top-down conspiracy;
McKay's rise to pre-eminence was simply the result of his being
too beloved to be reckoned with honestly. It's a Canadian fate.
In our interlocking food chains, your reputation precedes you,
though posterity may tarry.

At a wedding last summer in the Finger Lakes, where with some other guests I'd earlier delighted in local conspiracy theories about clandestine U.S. Naval experiments being conducted at the lake bottom, I found myself sidled up at the bar with another Canadian writer. We did what our kind does best: dredging. At one point my companion asked: 'So what ever happened to Steven Heighton?'

'What do you mean?'

'He was supposed to have been the next Ondaatje,' the writer said, referencing an early *Globe and Mail* review of Heighton's work. 'What happened?'

I got the hint. Despite being one of the most prolific, influential and talented Canadian writers of the last half-century, Heighton has never really made it on terms we Canadians understand. Sure, he's published five celebrated, award-winning works of fiction (bestsellers, critical crushes, a *New York Times* Book of the Year); five collections of poems influential to three generations of poets; and two books of essays—but who gives a damn? Ralph Fiennes never played one of Heighton's characters on the big screen. There's yet to be an Ang Lee joint. Heighton has never sententiously lobbied our prime minister to read more; he hasn't invented a remote book-signing robo-claw. We've never seen him in an ill-fitting tuxedo on CTV or CBC's Giller Prize step-and-repeat with Bob Rae or Rick Mercer. I know for a fact the guy's never stood in the Griffin Prize gala receiving line between Barbara Amiel and Michael Ignatieff. He hasn't even been the ship's doctor on one of Margaret Atwood's cruises! What in god's name happened?

The wedding guest might have alternately asked why it isn't conceivable for Heighton to receive the same treatment afforded Margaret Atwood, when a mixed review of her book of poems *The Door* was spiked by the very national newspaper that had commissioned it. Heighton, in other words, never got too big to fail. Instead, with the help of Palimpsest Press, he's now courting quite the opposite kind of attention by reissuing his out-of-print first book, the collection of poems *Stalin's Carnival*. Few Canadian writers of Heighton's stature and accomplishment would redirect our attention to their first effort. But why not go back and see for yourself where it all went wrong?

A warning: doing so may be confusing. Because from the very first line of its first poem, 'Endurance', *Stalin's Carnival* reveals itself to be a forgotten ur-text to what Canadian poetry has gotten right in the intervening years:

> At the crack she pounced
> hours over the grip of pool, she split
> the skin and sheered like a seawind back
> to breast the surface, ripple with fluid
> motion toward a standing wall.

Taking a cue from Layton's 'The Swimmer', with its verbal mimesis of muscling against hard going, 'Endurance' was swimming upstream against the poetic currents of 1989, a time that preferred the lazy river to the rapid. But 'Endurance' has endured. More of us sound more like Heighton in the water now than we do like Michael Ondaatje, floating frictionlessly along as he was on his '(Inner Tube)':

> On the warm July river
> head back

> upside down river
>
> for a roof
>
> slowly paddling
>
> towards an estuary between trees

When you write like Heighton can, you don't need sycophantic newspaper editors to do you favours. What's startling about *Stalin's Carnival* is how fully formed Heighton emerged. Some of his best and perennially anthologized poems are here, like 'High Jump' and 'The Machine Gunner'. And there are forgotten gems, too, such as 'On Reading Darwin' and 'A Perishable Art'. But what I'd forgotten was how unified the motion of the book is, how precise its thematic symmetry. It moves like its high jumper:

> Four strides the legs compass, close,
>
> burst gravity's shell and vault
>
> as sunrise at the pole bends
>
> back, sickles the sun-
>
> sleek arc of dolphin, diver, gull,
>
> his skull at noon and hovering.

Divided into three sections—the first songs of praise to the body and beauty, the second translations of, and meditations on, the poetry of Josef Stalin, the third the music of entropy and decay—*Stalin's Carnival* finds Heighton charting the metamorphoses of human energy into the antinomies that would preoccupy him for a lifetime: war and peace, east and west, Apollo and Dionysus, reason and faith, love and death. At the book's exact jet-black centre—page 47 of 95—we have Stalin recounting the midnight of the 20th century, his mercifully doomed pact with Hitler: 'It will be said that now truly I have no people/because in Hitler I had found a kind of brother.'

It would take another twenty-five years for Canadian poetry to catch up to the ambitious synthesis of sonic lushness and thematic unity that Heighton achieved in his first book. For comparison, check out other debuts—Ondaatje's *The Dainty Monsters* or Atwood's *Double Persephone*. Or rather, don't: the poems don't repay a second look. They didn't deserve a first look either. But each of those writers, by incarnating a nationalist bill of goods we were desperate to sell ourselves, were rushed into a sort of Twainian posterity that immediately made their poems too eminent to actually read. Heighton, fortunately, is just a writer. So what happened to him? Simple: his work stayed too good to be Great.

Thou: personal pronoun, 2nd person singular. Nominative (subjective case). Used familiarly, to an inferior, or in contempt. Archaic. It's the right title for Aisha Sasha John's second book, an apostrophe to people and places that are singular and contain solitudes, inaccessible to the first person—me. Hard to tell if it's being condescending. On the back cover, Michael Nardone says it's 'a sensing amid thought's most succulent folds'. No clue what that means. But I've heard gobbledygook like it before; it's aging badly.

Thou's two long poems—'Physical' and 'The Book of You'—descend into the cellar for the avant-garde's favourite dust-covered French vintage, the crisis of communicating. And they tackle the problem in the same old way, by straining against communicating. 'Physical' is set in Marrakesh where John was an artist in residence. It begins: 'I arrived here on Saturday./And today it is Monday.' There's livestock around—actually no: 'All of the cows. (No cows).' Maybe cows? Point is, it's hard to write about these things: places, people, the world. John, who has a gift for plotting that's sadly hampered in *Thou*, gets food poisoning almost immediately. She 'shat water/and barfed with unusual force.' Her kidneys hurt. How? 'It was physical.' Later, when the bug passes, John looks out at the moon and writes, 'I wasn't physical.' Then: 'I went upstairs and I was physical upstairs.' Last week the *Globe and Mail* excerpted a poem from the book about what it was like when John touched her own forehead. You guessed it: 'It's so easy and feels/feels so physical.' Later, she apologizes, sort of: 'I'm sorry I'm unsorry./(No I'm not. I am physical.)' No harm, no foul!

In case you're not getting the gist: things are physical and so they're not literal. You can't write about things, obvs. They're so physical that the word 'physical' and its adverbial variant are used, by my count, forty-four times in 'Physical'. John looks out at the world joyfully—she's fantastic at capturing her own excitement at being alive—but then just when we're about to be made to feel the thing that so excites her, we run up against the wall of her tired conceit. She writes: 'A story can be only one part.//Observing is all the analysis needed by anyone.'

What I always find suspect about a theoretical structure like John's—that the world is too physical to be transliterated faithfully—is that it gives the writer leave to abandon the difficult business of writing well. It's casuistry with a democratic function, giving writers not up to the challenge the excuse they require to produce literature stripped of its sole function: to communicate their world to another human being. John writes:

> I am as ordinary in my thinking as always.
> Nay, perhaps more so
> for I reach not
> into the stomach of my mind
> for that half-chewed image
> for which to surprise a you whom I imagine as the part of me
> that lives in others.
> For there is an Aisha in some
> bodies
> which allows them to be pleased
> in what I am pleased in.

In other words: John isn't going to bother regurgitating her experience of the world as the same old lyric pabulum. Aesthetic communication, if it isn't impossible, is inevitable. Even if the writing communicates nothing, to some it'll scan. Some people will just *get it* when John writes: 'Looking/like what one is is unavoidable and information/and physical.' John is saying that since no writing communicates, all writing communicates—especially the stuff you try the hardest to make the least communicative. The tautology provides that people who will like her writing will like her writing. And in a sense she's right; there's a whole coterie of 'experimental' types who will lap this stuff up, and the more undigested the better. But it's that sentiment itself that's premasticated, puked from beak to beak since Charles Mamma Bird Bernstein first barfed with unusual force.

What's so frustrating about *Thou* is that John is so much better than all this. She doesn't require the crutch of her conceit. When she isn't in a tailspin about its nature, John is brilliant at communicating. She's also really funny. Poems don't get more direct and precise and unforgettable than this:

> Frenchness is merely
>
> Britishness with a dab of
> butter and
> two winks.

In 'I keep sensing this child' she writes about a toddler at her hotel:

> George wouldn't jump into the pool because of my proximity to his
> father.
> So I said, Hi George. George is two but
> like, fuck George.
> Also, he gave me cut-eye.

Here in five short lines is a mini play, with distinct, effortlessly drawn characters in charming but real conflict. John has an ear tuned to our vernacular, capturing being surprised by 'a bunch of birds, three, several/birds, what the fuck', her phrasing a mimesis of the flutter and flash of both the birds and John's acrobatic mind. And 'The Book of You', which is less theoretically freighted than 'Physical', offers up some deceptively dashed-off urban portraits, reminiscent of Frank O'Hara, like 'On Bloor were two bike cops,' one of whom 'had too much air in his pants/where his bum could have been/not that I like/too much ass/on a man/still./I looked at their guns./The wind blew one's notepad down.//That's it.' Here is the counterevidence to John's conceit, her world captured and rapturously conveyed to a stranger.

Thou is a book by a writer whose best poems disprove her school's theories. John writes: 'I'm not going to suffer excellence.' I so wish she would.

INAUGURAL POEMS

The story goes he was blinded by the glare. And he was—you can tell even in the grainy monochromatic footage of John F. Kennedy's inauguration that the sun was bright on January 20th, 1961 in Washington. So bright that when an eighty-five-year-old Robert Frost—a long-standing supporter and friend of the president-elect—took the dais to read a poem he'd written for the occasion, Frost hesitated, stumbled as he strained to read, stopped, and instead recited a poem he'd written for no occasion but its own, with no palpable design upon us, and one he knew by heart: 'The Gift Outright.'

It's a better poem anyway. 'A Dedication', the poem Kennedy had commissioned Frost to write, isn't bad; if not necessarily by Frost's standards then surely by everybody else's. The opening, like the wood of an untravelled ship, groans in its new mooring: 'Summoning artists to participate/In the august occasions of the state/Seems something artists ought to celebrate.' Its redeeming virtue is that it ends unlike most occasional poems, whose authors tend to be too polite to spoil the mood they're charged to foster, on a note of ambivalence: 'A golden age of poetry and power/Of which this noonday's the beginning hour.'

Poetry and power don't comfortably (or frequently) intermingle, and Frost knew it. Noonday is the zenith, and a day is all decline and entropy from there. That may be why no other presidential inauguration featured a poet again until Clinton's first in 1993. There have been five poems read at five inaugurations: Frost's was the first, and then one at each of Clinton's and Obama's. Frost's invitation arose out of something of a historical curio. He had predicted that Kennedy would be the next President before Kennedy had even announced his candidacy, and his support for his young fellow New Englander wasn't lost on Kennedy; the two began a correspondence, and once Kennedy had in fact been elected, he called upon Frost to commemorate the occasion.

This had a vague political function. Frost was in 1961 the scion of an America that was already fading, a living link to the Protestant agrarian tradition that was giving way to the cosmopolitanism that Kennedy—young, Catholic, and with a promise of reform—heralded. Thus began the exclusively Democratic tradition of featuring an inaugural poet for political, if not necessarily literary, purchase.

Richard Blanco is the most recent installment, having read his painfully underwhelming poem 'One Today' at President Obama's second inauguration, this month [January 2013]. The poem brims with cliché, pat phrasing, and store-bought imagery. After the no-shit intro of 'The sun rose on us today', Blanco stumbles through an inexpertly enjambed stanza before arriving at 'My face, your face, millions of faces in morning's mirrors'. Next he deploys the unearned, inexact Newtown image of 'twenty children marked absent/today, and forever' to oblige us into fellowship. This is exactly what Keats complained about when he disparaged poems that have 'a palpable design upon us'. I feel sort of bad even writing about how bad it is. No, actually I don't. It's the worst.

But it does serve a very canny, even noble, political function. Blanco is gay, and he's Latino, and he's the youngest poet to ever read at an inauguration, and so his presentation acts as a set of policy gestures for the administration he's fêting. When he writes about his mother working a menial job 'for twenty years, so I could write this poem', the spirit of Horatio Alger is being inveighed, with its obligatory narrative of class ascendancy, and Obama can speak by proxy of his economic vision. They're the right policies, to be sure, but they're gestures made in the absence of the qualities of great literature: ambivalence, uncertainty, complication and nuance.

Occasional poetry is almost uniformly bad because it's an act of will, and not an act of grace. Poetry's power is its uselessness; as soon as it's employed in the service of an end, it's robbed of its wellspring. Auden: 'poetry makes nothing happen.' Even here there's a valuable double meaning. Poetry both does nothing and initiates the fertile, pre-cosmic state of un-being.

Yes, it was bright, and Frost was old. He was in front of his largest audience, an audience of millions, exceptional for any poet. And the day had been beset with weird distractions: at one point the podium caught fire as a Catholic bishop delivered a sonorous invocation, plasticky smoke rising up around him as if out of hell. But it could be too that the aging master, at the last second and in the noonlight of what matters, simply chose the better poem.

ROBERT FROST

Since the publication of Lawrence Thompson's three-volume biography of America's greatest poet, so much has depended on whether or not Robert Frost was a nice guy. This is due in part to Frost's popularity, but also to the fact that his clear, polished poems tempt many to see them as transparent—windows onto the mind of a simple Yankee farmer who spends his days worrying about birch fences and looking at spiders.

Thompson's book shattered the conception of Frost as a morally simple rural saint, depicting him instead as a grudge-ridden careerist, a neglectful husband and a skeptical father whose coolness to his son Carol's literary ambitions led, Thompson shamefully suggests, to Carol's suicide (Thompson has no qualms blaming Frost for the premature deaths of four of the poet's six children, including his three-year-old of cholera). Reviewing the biography in *The New York Times*, Helen Vendler famously called Frost 'a monster of egotism'. It's hard not to think that the neglect Frost's poetry suffered during the '70s and '80s, when his brand of deftly unadorned formalism fell into disrepute, had Thompson's biography to blame. America could accept *vers libre* from Ezra Pound, the fascist reactionary who offered the advice to 'make it new', howling madly about European Jewry's influence on international banking. But if that birch-swinging sonneteer Robert Frost turned out to have dissuaded his son from pursuing a career in poetry, that, my friends, was a bridge too far indeed.

Like most biographies, Thompson's tells us as much about its author as its subject. Thompson harboured an obsessive envy of Frost, and the two men pined for Frost's secretary after the death of Frost's wife. As a corrective, and to create a more sympathetic portrait, Donald Sheehy, Mark Richardson and Robert Faggen have teamed with Harvard University Press to publish the complete *Letters of Robert Frost*, a four-volume compendium of all of the poet's correspondence, the first volume of which is available now. The book starts with a 12-year-old Frost's love letter to his childhood sweetheart and ends with Frost touring his third and best book, *Mountain Interval*.

The hope is to have us meet the historical Frost on his own terms, as it were. Still, the fan who has 'The Road Not Taken' crocheted into his tea cozy might be in for a shock. To many readers Frost's poetry is an organic emanation of the American landscape from which it draws its inspiration, as wholesome and uncomplicated as a Vermont apple. The letters will revise that image. True, you won't find the cartoon villain of Thompson's biography—which Joyce Carol Oates recently parodied in her story 'Lovely, Dark, Deep'. But you will find a 20-year-old writing things like: 'Such an one am I that even in my failures I find all the promise I require to justify the astonishing magnitude of my ambitions.' The Frost of the letters is a prosody theorist, a scholar of Greek and Latin, a lazy and miserable farmer and, yes, a vain and self-conscious careerist brimming with ambition and ego. He was, after all, a poet.

In this first volume of letters, we get to see how that plainspoken sausage, for which Frost became so famous and misunderstood, gets made. It shouldn't be a surprise that it turns out it's an affected literary voice, nothing like Frost's erudite, widereferencing letters, which revel in multi-level puns and riddles as much as anything in Joyce. 'In North of Boston you are to see me performing in a language absolutely unliterary,' Frost writes in December 1913. 'What I would like is to get so I would never use a word or combination of words that I hadn't heard used in running speech.' But since we find no evidence in the letters that Frost's neighbours had the habit of speaking in masterful paragraphs of blank verse, or lived their lives, as Frost said of the poems in North of Boston, 'in a form suggested by the eclogues of Virgil,' we should take him at his word that these unselfconscious colloquialisms are actually rehearsed performances.

The sort of reader who thinks 'The Road Not Taken' is an unironic celebration of iconoclasm may also be surprised to find that Frost succumbed to bouts of nihilism, and even contemplated suicide. But they shouldn't be surprised. Lionel Trilling and Randall Jarrell both pointed out that Frost can be a deeply macabre poet. A sentiment of futility runs through many of his poems and occasionally erupts. It was Frost, after all, and not, say, Beckett, who wrote: 'The world is evil.' Frost is the fiendish brooder who bragged, 'I have been one acquainted with the night./I have walked out in the rain—and back in rain.' A poem like 'Out, Out', makes a spectacle of cruelty, revelling in the detail that a saw cuts off a farm boy's hand at the exact instant that his sister calls to him, 'Supper … As if to prove saws knew what supper meant.' Chillingly, the poem, as it has us gaze at the lifeless boy, says simply, 'No more to build on there,' as his family 'since they/were not the one dead, turned to their affairs.' And it was Frost who, through the voice of a mother who has just lost her first-born child, harangues the father (who may be Frost himself) in 'Home Burial': 'You could just sit there with the stains on your shoes/Of the fresh earth from your own baby's grave/And talk about your everyday concerns.' It's a *J'accuse* from Frost to himself, one that predates by half a century Thompson's allegations.

That's why I've never understood the scorn of Frost's critics. Vendler writes: 'Frost was, as John Berryman tells us, "The quirky medium of so many truths." The fact that his life validated scarcely any of those truths ... is a perplexity.' That's not a perplexity. It's a cliché. That so many perfect poems arose from an imperfect life isn't duplicity; it's grace.

IN PRAISE OF SHITTY TELEVISION

On Sunday, January 10, 2016, Ricky Gervais will host the 73rd annual Golden Globes, a performance for which he's already contrite. 'Because I can see the future,' Gervais tweeted, 'I'd like to apologise now for the things I said at next week's Golden Globes. I was drunk & didn't give a fuck.' But why stop the early *mea culpas* there? Someone—anyone—should pre-emptively apologise for the fact that Brad Pitt will show up, as is his wont, in those progressively transparent sunglasses that creep everyone out. Throw a 'my bad' to Bryan Cranston, who should have won Best Actor for his turn in *Trumbo*, but will lose to Leonardo DiCaprio (who will accept via video atop a human pyramid of supermodels on his yacht's helipad). And I'd like an apology from the Hollywood Foreign Press Association; they, like everyone else, still don't realize that bad television is better than good television.

To be fair, this year's televisual field is strong. *Empire*, *Game of Thrones*, *Mr. Robot*, *Narcos* and *Outlander* are nominated in the Drama category, while *Casual*, *Mozart in the Jungle*, *Orange Is the New Black*, *Silicon Valley*, *Transparent* and *Veep* are up for Best Musical or Comedy. But the best, most innovative and ubiquitous genre of TV show is conspicuously absent: reality TV. Whither *Bachelor in Paradise*, *Married at First Sight*, and *Naked and Afraid? Empire* is fine and all, but for real drama, watch Lifetime's *Born in the Wild* about, well, giving birth outside. And though *Orange Is the New Black* has its occasional droll moment, if you really want comedy tune into VH1's *Dating Naked*, which is—you guessed it—about courting in the buff.

In vogue right now though is so-called prestige TV—slick, voicey Millennial comedies like *Girls* and *Master of None*, and brooding dramas in the mould of *The Sopranos* and *Breaking Bad*. However finely crafted these shows may be, they're old news, essentially a long-form, serialized film, which itself evolved out of European theatre. Reality TV though is something completely new, one of those rare art forms that America invented whole-cloth, like Jazz, Abstract Expressionism, Rock & Roll, and Hip Hop. And like them, reality TV is susceptible to being written off as crass, stupid, immoral or innutritious by the cognoscenti.

Take for example the revered David Foster Wallace, whose essay 'E Unibus Pluram,' published a quarter century ago, endures as the most influential condescension to bad TV. The essay itself is like television: frantic, hysterical, then dull for long stretches, occasionally brilliant, and it goes on forever. It's quaintly dated now, with Wallace worrying himself into a panic over 'the advent of cable, often with packages of over forty channels', and the new 'remote control gizmo'. But to Wallace, TV posed a real, vexing problem to nothing less than American consciousness itself. The Cassandra of the boob tube, he warned that its 'weird pretty hand has my generation by the throat'. For Wallace, crappy television was immune to its own transcendence (this was the 90s, so naturally it was irony's fault), could adapt to and incorporate our anxieties about its badness, and therefore was unkillable.

In other words, David Foster Wallace was afraid of television. Being afraid of TV is fine I guess, but it's pretty much like being scared of your speaker system or your bookshelf. And of all the things that could really mess you up around the house, it makes a lot more sense to be spooked by your shower or your stairs. Because Wallace was writing long before our present

Golden Age of TV, it was television's badness he was afraid of, writing that, 'it's undeniable that television is an example of "low" art.' And I suspect that in our golden age, what people dislike about reality TV is its perceived baseness, its cast of vain and stupid and beautiful people, its lack of *serious* writers and directors behind the scenes, its cloying, shiny eagerness to please. What people like about prestige television is that it's TV that's least like itself (and more like film or theatre). But that precisely is television's genius: that whereas most art ends up only being what it isn't, bad TV is so good at being exactly what it is. But reality TV is bad in the old fashioned way that television used to be bad, and not, say, in the innovative, *avant-garde* way that *True Detective* season 2 is bad.

Keep in mind that reality television is not being made by stupid people. Whereas not too long ago, artistic young men and women of talent and ambition would move to Paris to write novels and poems, now they move to Burbank to produce *The Bachelor*. Don't let Teresa Giudice's hairline fool you; highbrow things are happening in reality TV. It was born on June 28th, 1947, and on the radio. At 7:30 that evening Allen Funt debuted his show *The Candid Microphone*, where he'd put regular people in bizarre, infuriating situations, and then at the nadir of their befuddlement, he'd reveal that they were being taped. Within a year, the show had moved to television and been renamed *Candid Camera*.

With its elegant, delightful volta—'Smile, you're on *Candid Camera!*'—Funt's show was the sonnet that launched the Elizabethan Renaissance that is modern reality television. It's as American an invention as any: low-cost, franchisable, revolutionary, by the people, for the people. Of all its innovations, maybe its most fascinating is how it's troubled our conception of acting. As the title of Funt's show suggests, reality TV—and its

viewership—is obsessed with candor. Candor too was the obsession of the last revolutionary movement in acting before reality
TV came along, the Stanislavski/Adler Method made famous
by Marlon Brando. The Method, as it was later known, was a
way for actors not to approximate feelings, but to have them.
The day that *The Candid Microphone* premiered, Funt made
Stanislavski and Adler's technology obsolete.

Though what reality TV skeptics complain about most frequently is that the shows, and the people on them, are 'fake'. By
fake, they mean that the casts of everything from *Road Rules* to
the sadly defunct *Here Comes Honey Boo Boo* are either being
socially engineered to behave telegenically, or else are themselves hamming it up. But that's to utterly miss the point; it's
like complaining about Brando staying in character between
takes in *Apocalypse Now*. Like the method actor, Funt figured
out how to engineer candor, but in other people instead of himself. If the method actor was a kind of virtuoso soloist, the post-
Funt reality TV producer is a master conductor, playing the
entire orchestra of her cast at once, monitoring rushes, keeping
them up all night, confiscating their books and phones, drench-
ing everything in alcohol, all in order to bore, piss off and
seduce real human beings into delivering the performance of
their lives.

And of course in those performances they're playing themselves. This is the other deep revelation of reality television, that
our own personality is a performance, one that's actualized by
an audience. F. Scott Fitzgerald called personality nothing more
than a series of successful gestures, and he'd never even seen
Married by Mom and Dad. And the reality TV on-camera interview, sometimes called 'in-the-moments', where contestants
address the camera directly to brag, blame and bloviate, are
doing to television what Shakespeare's soliloquies did to

literature: giving characters a confessor, and giving audiences exclusive access to a mind that opens only when it's observed.

In our golden age, we want TV to be a fine wine, when its spirit, its genius is closer to Appalachian moonshine—wild, crazy-making, and a little naughty. Maybe the best testament to reality TV's revolutionary power was in 1969, when an Eastern Airlines flight from Newark to Miami was hijacked. 'Ladies and gentlemen,' the captain announced over the intercom, 'we've got a man up here that wants to go to Havana, so we're going to Cuba.' The frumpy hijacker, in an ill-fitting suit, held a knife to the flight attendant's throat almost comically. But passengers soon noticed that on board with them was a sombre Allen Funt. Instantly the mood lightened—to the pudgy hijacker's chagrin—and despite Funt's protestations that they were not in fact on *Candid Camera*, the passengers gave the hijacker a standing ovation when they touched down.

On a perfectly serviceable night in 2014, 13.5 million North Americans—a plurality of the television audience that night—tuned in to watch Tommy Chong dance a cha-cha to 'Drop It Like It's Hot'. Lea Thompson, the mom from *Back to the Future*, tried to wind back the clock of her career with a foxtrot. Carlton from *The Fresh Prince of Bel-Air*, someone named Alfonso Ribeiro, declared 'there's more to me than just Carlton', before executing a frantic jive. Across the continent, we blushed like so many autumn leaves; *Dancing with the Stars* is back.

Dancing with the Stars isn't good television; it isn't even good bad television. But it's necessary television. There are people who say they watch it for the dancing, which is about as convincing as an ancient Roman saying she watches the Colosseum's gladiatorial games for the costumes. It's the cruellest show on television, the 'Stars' of its title laden with irony, as it snares our culture's has-beens, aren't-quite-yets, and never-weres and gets them to dance—literally dance—for their lives.

In the Byzantine, articulated digestive tract of celebrity culture, *Dancing with the Stars* is the ignoble terminus. Its contestants, for whom we were once so hungry, have wended their way through our culture's dark channels, and are now unceremoniously dropped onto the repository of its stage for one last laugh. The presence of host Tom Bergeron, known best for helming *America's Funniest Home Videos*, alerts viewers to the fact that any humour generated by the show is at the contestants' expense.

A load-bearing pillar of the show's pathetic poetry is the aesthetic rigour of its judging panel, the snobbiest of any such panel on television. Whereas *American Idol*'s panel confines its criticism to the vague personal impressions of its judges, the panel on *Dancing with the Stars* goes in for close readings, all but putting a protractor to turn-out angles, and a level to each *port de bras.* People who used to be famous perform dances that used to be popular, and viewers can vote the stars back into obscurity by dialling a 1-800 number that, at least for the stars, isn't entirely toll free.

If *Dancing with the Stars* didn't exist, we would have to invent it. It serves an essential function in celebrity culture, to let us condescend to the stars to whom we so often aspire. Where else can we turn to see Betsey Johnson, looking heavily medicated, ensnare her feet in a pink boa she herself designed while cha-chaing to 'Material Girl'? Whither can we turn to see Daytona 500 champion Michael Waltrip—with a self-described 'ass like a pair of cats wrastlin' in a bag'—lurch jerkily to 'Born to Be Wild'? Aside from a furtively captured, drunken hamburger-eating session, or leaked elevator video, there's nowhere else to see those who were once so mighty rendered so low.

In that way, *Dancing with the Stars* bears more than a passing resemblance to what Aristotle thought tragedy was—hubris conquered by nemesis, and the reversal of fortune of the once mighty. The aesthetic pleasure the show generates—which is a lot for such an awful, cruel show—is the same purgative pity and fear we feel watching Oedipus realize his marriage to Jocasta isn't as uncomplicated as he'd thought. The show is the next-to-final moment in a classical tragedy, the moment just before the hero's *anagnorisis*, or recognition of catastrophe. Everyone knows that the last our culture will ever see of MMA fighter Randy Couture is him waltzing to 'The Way You Look Tonight'—everyone except Randy Couture.

And so before he took the stage to foxtrot, dressed like one of the patrons of the bar on *Star Trek: TNG*, journalist Tavis Smiley captured the import of the moment when he said: 'People know the some of us, but not the sum of us.' Here assembled are yesteryear's journeymen of celebrity culture, short on time and long on hope, ready for one last dance for all the marbles. Their heydays are long since passed, their revels all but ended. Their fate will be determined by their ability to execute a technical challenge that only perfection can keep from looking funny, a brass tacks redress to the randomness of fame. Vaseline those teeth, suck in that gut, and dance, monkey, dance.

TRAILER PARK BOYS

Legend has it that the Canadian word 'hoser', the pejorative portmanteau made popular by SCTV's Bob and Doug McKenzie, may have originated when some snobby citiot caught a couple of guys down on their luck siphoning gas out of a car. *Trailer Park Boys*, the beloved Canadian television show that dilates on the fictional RV community of Sunnyvale, Nova Scotia, is an extended study of the hoser conducted with the discernment of a connoisseur. In fact, in an episode from the show's third season, Ricky, Julian and Bubbles open a gas station in the park supplied entirely by siphoned gas. When asked how to tell one grade of gas from another, Ricky, the sommelier of hosers, snaps back: 'What are you stupid? You f*****g taste it. Unleaded tastes a little tangy; supreme is kinda sour; and diesel tastes pretty good.'

Netflix resurrected *Trailer Park Boys* and premiered a new season, the show's eighth, and the new season finds the characters where we left them, a little puffier but undiminished, doing what they do best—getting drunk and high, as Ricky might put it, and cobbling together an illegal and almost thought-through scheme to make some money and save the trailer park. Besides the fact that Jonathan Torrens seems sadly to have forgotten how to play J-Roc, the eighth season is mostly a return to form, and fans will recognizing some familiar tropes: Bubbles has a new cat-themed entrepreneurial foray; there's some face-saving pet-swapping by subterfuge; a new batch of Ricky's delicious spoonerisms and solecisms; and of course, a hazy plan to get rich selling dope.

Back too is the sense that *Trailer Park Boys*, for all its

salaciousness, may very well be the most moral show on television. When we first meet our heroes, Ricky and Julian, they're in a gunfight over a Pomeranian. But like all of their gunfights, no one (save Ricky occasionally) ever seems to get hurt. It's the first of many of the rules of *Trailer Park Boys*, that you can live a good and moral life by: sure, you can get yourself into a shootout, but don't actually shoot someone. Later Julian decides that he needs space from Ricky, whose bumbling, as usual, sent them both to jail. But when there's nowhere for Ricky to spend the night, Julian, the consummate friend, offers him his porch and a snack. Here's another of those rules you can live by: when the buddy who sent you to jail needs to crash on your front steps, the least you can do is offer him some vodka and raw hot dogs. Glossing every crime is a kindness that feels uniquely Canadian and collectivist; it's Maury Povich meets Tommy Douglas.

The moral universe of *Trailer Park Boys* couldn't be in starker relief to those of the major dramas and comedies of our time. Whether it's *Breaking Bad* or *Curb Your Enthusiasm*, most American television of the 21st century has offered up characters who are selfish to the point of psychopathy. Even Louis C.K., a moral leader in American comedy, offers a vision of the world that's sweetly nihilistic. Beckett meets Charlie Brown, where if the selfish don't necessarily always succeed, at least they try. The guys on *Trailer Park Boys* may misbehave, but their criminality is never allowed to trespass upon other people's feelings. In one episode, when both Ricky and his daughter Trinity are trying to quit smoking together, Ricky teaches us an important lesson in selfless parenting: if you steal the last of your nine-year-old kid's Nicorette patches, it's only fair when she wakes you up the next morning on the hood of your car clutching a vodka bottle, that you tear the patch in half and split it with her. Whereas American television is about good guys breaking bad, *Trailer Park Boys* is about bad guys breaking good.

Look no further than how the boys treat their hostages. Sure, Julian may have a penchant for abducting famous Canadian musicians, but it's usually for a higher cause. When they hijack Rita MacNeil's tour van and use her and her band's slave labour to harvest their four thousand marijuana plants, Bubbles turns to remonstrate Ricky: 'You're forcing Rita MacNeil and her band to harvest dope at gunpoint: you could be a little f*****g nicer about.' After Lahey and Randy trick Bubbles out of his Rush concert tickets, Ricky, to console his best friend, abducts Alex Lifeson from his hotel room for a private concert in duct tape shackles. 'This isn't kidnapping,' Ricky consoles Lifeson, 'I'm just borrowing you for a little bit.' As they pull into Sunnyvale, the Rush guitarist asks Ricky where they are. 'F*****g best trailer park in the goddamn world. Good people, good friends.'

And so in a television landscape where capitalist self-interest rules, and the moral landscape is darkening to pitch, *Trailer Park Boys* stands out once again as an unlikely moral beacon, the hoser an unlikely hero. In season eight, the fate of Sunnyvale is once again in the balance, and saving the good, sweet place may require the Bubbles in all of us to transform our cat-themed Shed and Breakfast into a house of prostitution. The hosers are asked once more to do the right thing, the Canadian thing, for the greater good. Then get drunk and high.

For Hemingway, all a bar needed to succeed was good lighting, 'a certain cleanliness and order', and no music. To Jon Taffer, the food and beverage consultant and impresario behind *Bar Rescue*, Hemingway, no greenhorn to the gin mill, didn't know the half of it.

In the opening credits of *Bar Rescue*, a voice announces: 'Running a bar is not just a business; it's a science.' In each episode, Taffer tackles the business first, descending on each ailing drinkery to fire its dishonest staff, rehabilitate its incompetent managers, and shame its lecherous owners. He'll balance your books, bring down your beverage cost and get all up in your grill about an unsanitary kitchen, his Long Island baritone scaling into an indignant quack (Sunday saw him warm to a neologism for a bacteria colony in a freezer—a s***sicle).

But after he's redesigned a bar's menu and run it through a service stress test, the show departs from its genre conventions and ventures into the 'science' of bar culture. The science comes from Taffer's reverse engineering of America's most successful bars and restaurants, best practices that run the gamut from the sage to the insane. In every area of a bar's redesign, he eschews taste for statistics. Bar stools should be a certain height and distance from each other to optimize sociability and drink consumption. Pool tables should only ever be lit with incandescent light, because fluorescent fixtures tire the eye and reduce time played and beverages bought. Bars with dance floors should feature the felicitously named 'butt funnel', an architectural bottle neck that squeezes patrons into close encounters of the lucrative kind, resulting in a 15 percent increase in the ratio of beers slammed per rug cut.

Taffer's social scientism therefore owes a debt to one of today's most popular and divisive public intellectuals, Malcolm Gladwell. Both Taffer and Gladwell mine social history, which had previously only been explicable by qualitative argument, for behaviours that can be synthesized into quantitative laws as ironclad as those of physics. To Taffer, drinkers are no more than complex—albeit sluggish—particles, whose patterns are not just intelligible, but replicable. The people who serve them aren't bartenders; they're mixologists. To Gladwell's Law of the Few and Stickiness Factor, Taffer, in trying to manufacture the Gladwellian Tipping Point in the bars he rescues, offers the Law of the Stool and the Butt Funnel Factor.

And so in Taffer's renovated bars, we can see what Gladwellian social scientism looks like in brick and mortar. The renovations are machine-tooled for economic effect. The sightlines are paved towards the premium liquor brand bottles incandescently lit for maximal thirst induction. Seat cushion travel is algorithmically calibrated for optimal wallet disbursement. And in the freezer of a hip-hop club Taffer renovated (I wish I was making this up), soaked and frozen hand towels have been stacked for the easy application to the necks of fighting female patrons, 'cold tasers', tooled to an ideal 'cat-fight'-dispersal to law-suit-avoidance ratio.

In other words, there's a creepy calculatedness to the renovations on *Bar Rescue*, and the cumulative effect of all that subliminal scientism is, to quote the poet John Keats, 'a palpable design on us'. In a split-screen the afters at first glance fare better than the befores, but on close inspection there's an ineffable feeling that each detail has traded its charm for statistical significance, and that what once made each successful has been rendered uncanny when collated, crunched and reverse engineered. The transformed bars all have the cynical look of home-grown Milestones or Kelsey's waiting to go viral, a Frankenbar of the tried and tested. In the Gladwellian calculus of culture, things become not the sum, but the difference, of their parts.

And yet when you zoom out, *Bar Rescue* itself is assembled much the same way. But it works. It's as if Taffer and his producers sat down with the Neilson ratings to see how many of the top shows they could squeeze into theirs. Nested in *Bar Rescue* are a cooking show, a financial management show, and a renovation show, all housed within a redemptive arc with a Gordon Ramsay screamer type thrown in for good measure. I've watched every single episode. Being played so well never felt so good.

And anyways, there's no use getting worked up about it; this is what the future looks like. Ours is a moment that hasn't yet reached its apogee, the simultaneous rise of the Gladwellian social scientist and the consultant, both of whom may be short on vision, but are long on data. Time was that all a bar proprietor—or a showrunner—had to lure in customers was imagination, that analogue predecessor of the algorithm. But who needs imagination when you have Google Analytics?

THE LEFTOVERS

There's a mysterious hole at the centre of HBO's new sci-fi drama *The Leftovers*, but it's not the one you're thinking of. The one you're thinking of is the Disappearance, the Rapture-like event when, on October fourteenth, 2 percent of humanity inexplicably vanished. Set in the sleepy hamlet of Mapleton, New York, *The Leftovers* dilates on a group of inter-connected characters as they struggle to make sense of a world suddenly as inscrutable, contradictory and meaningless as the world of *Ecclesiastes* (both the Pope and Gary Busey pulled a Houdini on the fourteenth).

Coming as it does from *Lost* co-creator Damon Lindelof, it would be safe to assume that *The Leftovers* is working towards the final revelation of the science behind its science fiction, but the show makes clear early that it isn't much interested in the nature of the Disappearance. In a tart bit of dramatic irony, October fourteenth is the day of Mapleton High School's Science Fair, where police chief Kevin Garvey's daughter, Jill, is giving a presentation on entropy, the universe's tendency towards increasing chaos. And in one of the early episodes, a group of the world's top scientists delivers a report on The Disappearance to a U.S. Senate committee where they conclude, that, er, they don't know what the hell happened. 'Say not thou, "What is the cause that the former days were better than these?" for thou dost not inquire wisely concerning this' —Ecclesiastes 7:10.

While there may be a dearth of answers from the scientific community about what happened, there is, as usual, no shortage of charlatans with all the answers, so many in fact that the Bureau of Alcohol, Tobacco and Firearms, the ATF, has tacked on an extra letter to their acronym for their newest beat in the Great Tribulation—a 'C', for 'Cults'. But the two leading cults couldn't have more different world views. The dourer of the two is the Guilty Remnant, a mirthless band of silent chain-smoking stalkers in white smocks ('Let thy garments always be white' —Ecclesiastes 9:8) led by the smoldering zealot Patti Levin. The Guilty Remnant dragoon Chief Garvey's wife, Laurie, and later, their daughter, Jill, heartbroken over Laurie's absence. Their mission is to remind the world of the Disappearance by standing silent vigil outside people's homes, or breaking into them and stealing photos of their raptured loved ones, and they so renounce the world that they allow their members to be martyrs. The other cult, which attracts the Garveys' son, is led by the earthy Holy Wayne, a lightly shirted man with a soft spot for young Asian women who, for a price, will help you forget your pain with a hug and a few whispered words from *Ecclesiastes* ('For whoever is joined with all the living, there is hope; surely a live dog is better than a dead lion'). His followers don't play the martyr game; when the ATFC come calling, they answer the door with their guns.

Viewers of the show, like its characters and its cults, can interpret almost everything that happens in *The Leftovers* through these two lenses, as either pointing back to the supernatural or forward to the secular. When the future leader of the Guilty Remnant, Patti, confesses to her therapist and future acolyte Laurie Garvey that she has a feeling that 'the world is going to end', is it a premonition of the Disappearance that is only a day away, or a surfeit of anxiety caused by her abusive relationship? Are Kevin Garvey's father's ravings oracular, heavy with portent, or simply the emanations of an ill mind? When a bird lands on a hot roulette table, is it a sign of anything more than an open window in the casino? Like *Ecclesiastes*, the world of *The Leftovers* can be read one of two ways: as a nihilistic vale of tears ('all is vanity') or as a stage for earthly hope ('I said in my heart, "Go now, I will prove thee with mirth."')

What determines which direction a character—and a viewer—will break is whether she is willing to forget the catastrophe at the show's centre. Whereas *Lost* was about solving the mystery at its heart, *The Leftovers* is about outliving it. The great disappearance at the centre of *The Leftovers* is not the 2 percent of humanity that has inexplicably disappeared, furnishing the show with its concept and its world with grief; instead, it's the show's genre itself that, over the course of its first season, is slowly vanishing. *The Leftovers* is science-fiction television whose sci-fi is being raptured before our eyes. Unlike *Lost*, the mechanics of the mystery at the show's centre isn't germane to anyone other than the Guilty Remnant. To the hopeful, *The Leftovers* is about uncovering a deeper mystery: how to go on living.

For all the ink that has been spilled about the bleakness of the show, those who haven't given up on it can see it's trending towards the light. The central conflict, in the face of illegible loss, is whether its characters read into the Disappearance either the Guilty Remnant's message of neurotic nihilism, or Holy Wayne's earthly hope. Hope looks like it's winning. Nora Durst, whose pain at losing her entire family was so intense that she'd still shop for their favourite food, now, after a hug from Holy Wayne, shops for herself. In the show's most exquisite scene yet, last night Laurie broke her vow of silence to scream her daughter's name to her estranged husband, Kevin, to alert him to the fact that Jill was trapped in the Guilty Remnant's burning house. And now a crop of newborns that Wayne sired is being left on people's doorsteps in a kind of anti-rapture. Ultimately *The Leftovers* isn't about the mystery of tragedy, but the mystery of hope, which is as much an act of will as an act of god. 'One generation passeth away, and another generation cometh; but the earth abideth forever.'

What does it mean to kill a zombie? The answer, like the enemy, is a no-brainer. In AMC's *The Walking Dead*, equivocating on the question is at best a sign of mental weakness, and at worst of moral perversion. To the survivor of the zombie apocalypse, it means no more and no less than one fewer walker, biter or geek.

It's worth noting, though, that the original fear related to the zombie isn't of being attacked by one, but of becoming one. The idea of the zombie has its roots in Congolese mythology, but finds its mature expression in Haitian religious thinking, where it's a metaphor for slavery, the soul evacuated from the body, the will domesticated by the magic of the witch doctor, who uses the zombie to do his bidding. With the reprieve of death interrupted, it's the fear of an afterlife of penury, instead of paradise. In other words, in Haiti, we're meant to empathize with the zombie, pity his fate and fear it for ourselves.

When the metaphor is reanimated in America, not long after it has convulsed in an apocalyptic battle over slavery, the perspective has tellingly changed. 1932's *White Zombie* is the first feature-length zombie film, and in it a white Haitian plantation owner enlists his neighbour—a voodoo master and owner of a sugar cane plantation run by zombie slave labour—to help him turn his female houseguest into his zombie bride. The climax comes when her fiancée has to fight off being overwhelmed by a zombie hoard. Transposed to America, the zombie anxiety is less a pitiable personal fate as it is the fear of a slave insurrection.

The zombies we all know today were invented by George Romero in 1968's *Night of the Living Dead*. For the most part, the racial overtones of the zombie myth's Haitian origin have been dissolved, though *Night of the Living Dead* does take place in rural Pennsylvania, not far from Gettysburg, where America fought to save its soul. Romero established many of the tropes that went on to define modern zombies, the lumbering, flesh-hungry reanimated corpses that swarm the living. Societal breakdown is a major anxiety, as the insurrection can be passed through infected mouths. It was ahead of its time in that it starred a white actress (Judith O'Dea) paired controversially with a black actor (Duane Jones). But after Jones has survived the zombie onslaught, in a darkly ironic turn he's killed by his emancipators, a posse of good ol' boys who take him for a zombie and shoot him on sight. This is 1968, the year that Martin Luther King Jr. is murdered.

To Romero, though, who is to zombie films what Petrarch was to sonnets, his new genre is plastic, malleable, and gives him room to ask how we should feel about zombies, and about killing them. His *Day of the Dead* (1985) features a kind of zombie hero, Bub, played humanely by Sherman Howard, who listens to Beethoven as his face contorts in baffled ecstasy, remembers bits and pieces of his life, and can shoot a gun. It's radical: The director who first made us fear zombies has, 20 years later, made us empathize with one.

By the time we get to *The Walking Dead*, the most popular iteration of the genre, Romero's geometric zombie has been made linear again. In its world of violent pragmatism, anything but murderous resolve toward the zombie is a symptom of intellectual or mental illness. In the show's second season, when they arrive on Hershel's farm, the group discovers that the kindly veterinarian Hershel, the show's moral leader, is keeping a group of zombified loved ones in his barn. He's holding out for a cure, but Rick and his crew see Hershel's empathy as a dangerous luxury belonging to a bygone, morally decadent time. Hershel's nemesis, the man who eventually murders him, the psychopathic Governor, is beset by Hershel's same misapprehension; he keeps his zombie daughter alive in a straitjacket, and snuggles with her before bed. The governor's vestigial empathy is a symbol of the danger of his nostalgic utopianism, and in a kind of grim symmetry, both men meet their end on the same day.

Can a metaphor shed its political origins? In America, zombies have been an empty receptacle for so many of its anxieties: collective bargaining, consumerism, foreign invasion, pandemics. But what about slavery? Considering its origin in the Haitian nightmare of slavery, it's hard not to think that *The Walking Dead*'s grimly pragmatic recasting of the metaphor is, as they say, problematic. *The Walking Dead* takes place in the American South, in and around Atlanta. One season sees the gang of survivors, headed by a white Southern lawman, holed up in an exquisite Georgian farmhouse. In another season, they expropriate a prison. Both are symbols of America's historical inequities.

Maybe most disturbing of all is how in the zombie becoming the perfect villain—unnuanced, insatiable and undeserving of empathy—it also becomes the perfect victim. In *The Walking Dead*, the nightmare of reanimated man is also the dream of violence vindicated. Violence against zombies is stripped of its sociological and political reality, and exists in a state of pragmatic self-justification. It is no less fraught than cutting the grass, an automatic routine performed with a blank expression. The show's lengthy disquisitions on the need for unfussy pragmatism reinforce the fact that *The Walking Dead* is a kind of libertarian fantasy, a moral wash into which ethical questions about violence dissolve in a bath of self-preservation.

The Walking Dead may be the most popular zombie franchise, but it's far from the best. Its unselfconscious handling of a racially fraught metaphor and its orgiastic embrace of violence make it frivolous in its self-seriousness. For my money, the best zombie vehicle is 2004's endlessly clever *Shaun of the Dead*, where the zombie represents the British work-a-day routine ever-so-slightly upended, giving the title character a new shape and meaning to his life. And tellingly, Shaun's loved ones who turn into zombies are treated with a pathos and dignity that recall the myth's Haitian origins. All brawn, what *The Walking Dead* lacks is what zombies themselves keep demanding: BRAINS.

———————

Old Dixie wasn't driven down at night, but rather at first light on April 3, 1865, when the Twenty-Fifth Corps of the Union Army, an all-black formation, broke from their lines and marched on Richmond, the Confederate capital left undefended after General Robert E. Lee had ordered what remained of the Army of Northern Virginia to retreat towards Appomattox. The Corps' 9th Regiment marched into the streets, singing 'John Brown's Body'. Black residents of the city lined the streets and cheered and wept, rang the city bells and joined in the song, so yes, 'all the bells were ringing,/The night they drove Old Dixie Down,/And all the people were singing.'

What a coup: the greatest song about the American Civil War of the past 100 years (a song told from the perspective of a Southern soldier) was written by a half-Jewish, half-Mohawk kid from Toronto, Robbie Robertson. Let's get the nitpicking out of the way first. Yes, there are historical inaccuracies in 'The Night They Drove Old Dixie Down'. There's no way that Virgil Caine, the Confederate soldier in whose voice the song is sung, could have returned home to his wife in Tennessee, who one day called to him and said, '"Virgil, quick, come and see, there goes Robert E. Lee."' Lee had by then surrendered to Ulysses S. Grant—who on that fateful day was suffering from an intense migraine—at the home of Wilmer McLean in the village of Appomattox Courthouse, Virginia. Joan Baez, the story goes, pointed that out to Robertson, who then changed the lyrics to 'there goes the *Robert E. Lee*', as in CSS *Robert E. Lee*, the Confederate warship. That doesn't fix the problem, though, as CSS *Robert E. Lee* was run down and captured by USS *James Adger* near Bermuda on November 9, 1863.

But it doesn't really matter because it's such a great goddamn line, such an amazing verse, such an unbearably beautiful song. It's a bit of magic, the sort of magic that in my opinion even the great Gordon Lightfoot never managed to summon in historical ballads like 'The Wreck of the Edmund Fitzgerald' or 'The Canadian Railroad Trilogy'. Here not only is the wonder and respect of the minor historical character rendered perfectly and in an economical, idiomatic way, but so too is the object of the character's admiration, Lee himself. You can almost see him riding slowly and sadly and still dignified through the broken streets on his huge white horse, Traveller. You can almost hear, too, the ethos of the man who, when offered command of the Union Army by Abraham Lincoln, refused it to fight against the country he loved on behalf of his home state of Virginia, which he loved even more. E. M. Forster wrote: 'If I had to choose between betraying my country and betraying my friend, I hope I should have the guts to betray my country.'

If you put a gun to my head and asked who wrote a better line about bells, Gerard Manley Hopkins or Robbie Robertson, I'd have to go with Robertson. Hopkins's famous line is 'each hung bell's/Bow swung finds tongue to fling out broad its name.' Robertson's is simply 'and all the bells were ringing'. This is something I wish Canadian poets would pick up on: The former predicts it, the later performs it. The bell finds its tongue in the clean, mournful ringing of Robertson's heavy brass line, and not the wind-chiming mania of Hopkins's.

More importantly, Robertson achieves in 'The Night They Drove Old Dixie Down' what the very best histories of the war (I'm thinking of John Keegan's *The American Civil War* and Shelby Foote's *The Civil War*) can only hint at: the particular admixture of defeat and pride, dignity and shame, that distinguished the Confederate soul. The song captures the terrible and defiant and beautiful sense that history is rightly against the Confederates, and that they hate history for it. It's almost as if Robertson and The Band took Faulkner's famous paragraph about Pickett's Charge and transposed it into song (a song which, by the way, Levon Helm, a Southerner himself, refused ever to sing again after his heartbreaking performance of it during *The Last Waltz*):

'Maybe this time with all this much to lose and all this much to gain: Pennsylvania, Maryland, the world, the golden dome of Washington itself to crown with desperate and unbelievable victory the desperate gamble, the cast made two years ago....'

I'MMA LET YOU FINISH, BUT KANYE IS THE GREATEST CRITIC OF OUR TIME

Like our own Star of Bethlehem, the heavenly body to which our Magi move, it was Kim Kardashian who announced the December birth of her son, in a tweet: 'Saint West'. But his name has Kanye written all over it. With a daughter named North, christening his son after another cardinal direction would have smacked too much of a sequel and Kanye has forgone franchises since naming his trilogy—*The College Dropout*, *Late Registration* and *Graduation*—after post-secondary education. Plus if you're the guy who bragged 'I am a God', naming your kid after a heavenly caste is a no-brainer, though there are scant few— Seraphim? Archangel?—that you can coo into a bassinet.

The tell though is in the editorializing, its rejoinder to *Pulp Fiction*'s Butch who says: 'I'm an American honey. Our names don't mean shit.' *Saint* West: Kanye gave his son an honorific where a given name should go. Instead of a sobriquet, he gave a first impression. In other words, he critiqued. What else would we expect from a man so constitutionally incapable of holding his tongue, whose pronouncements and opining have had a cultural impact equal to his art, maybe more? Kanye has emerged as one of those rare, benighted artist-critics, like Randall Jarrell, Renata Adler, David Foster Wallace, maybe even George Orwell, who turn our heads more easily with their essays than their art. Saint will forever have his father's divine judgement baked into his name, so that even as your tongue forms the sibilant to pronounce it, a figure rises, snatches the mic and says: Saint, I'mma let you finish, but Kanye is the greatest critic of our time.

And he actually is. He isn't the *best* critic of our time—that's Renata Adler, Clive James, Camille Paglia, Stephen Metcalf, Laura Kipnis or Ta-Nehisi Coates, depending who you ask—but Kanye is the greatest. His critiques are international events, endlessly parsed, scoffed at, argued about and memed. Sure it's easy to think of his public decrees as the unselfconscious bloviating of an egomaniac—his habit of advertising which intoxicant is fuelling each outburst doesn't help—but as far as I can tell, he's also the only critic in the history of the United States whose comments have elicited a response from two sitting presidents. You can't say the same thing about Edmund Wilson. Number 43 called Kanye's famous 'George Bush doesn't care about black people' comment the 'all-time low' of his presidency (9/11 and 'Mission Accomplished' are runners-up, surely), and Barack Obama, after the Taylor Swift incident, called Kanye a 'jackass'.

In his book *The Origins of Criticism*, a study of the rise of critical culture in ancient Greece, Andrew Ford defines criticism as 'any public act of praise or blame'. Ford argues that before the fourth century BCE, when criticism became its own discipline, it would have followed any public performance. Art and critique occurred inseparably. Ford quotes George Kennedy's introduction to the *Cambridge History of Literary Criticism*: 'Criticism as an instinctive reaction to the performance of poetry is as old as song.'

That makes Kanye West a contemporary avatar of the ancient, original critic, whose two cents are always on offer (especially if you've had 'a little sippy sippy', as Kanye confessed he'd had before the 2006 MTV Europe Video Music Awards, when, miffed that he hadn't won video of the year, he took to the stage to rave: 'Oh hell no. This video cost a million dollars. I had Pam Anderson. I was jumpin across canyons and shit.') His venue is the live performance, and most frequently, the awards show. But Kanye's choice of medium is one of the aspects of his criticism that people most dislike. After Kanye put George Bush on blast during the Katrina relief telethon, host Matt Lauer said: 'Emotions in this country right now are running very high. Sometimes that emotion is translated into inspiration, sometimes into criticism.' NBC decided to edit the comment out of its West Coast feed. A statement from the network read: 'It would be most unfortunate if the efforts of the artists who participated tonight ... are overshadowed by one person's opinion.'

That's exactly what had happened, thank god; no one today remembers any of the telethon except for that 'one person's opinion'. What America wanted—needed—to talk about was precisely what Kanye had maybe indelicately proposed: that the federal government may have acted more quickly and comprehensively had the hurricane struck a city that was more predominately white. The fact that NBC executives thought that as New Orleans lay broken, the country should instead focus its attention on Faith Hill's anaemic performance of 'Precious Lord, Take My Hand', is proof of how necessary Kanye's intervention was.

It's Kanye's critiques at awards shows that really piss people off, and for the same reason that NBC condemned and redacted his Bush comment during the telethon: that it's self-absorbed to interrupt the preordained, unbroken draft of cultural capital with one person's opinion. His critical career began in 2004, when he stormed out of the American Music Awards in protest after losing Best New Artist to Gretchen Wilson. When asked about the incident, he said: 'I'm speaking about it as a fan of hip hop. If somebody asked me: what do you think is the biggest thing in hip hop in 2004, and if I say "me", it comes off as arrogant to people. But my confidence and their lack of esteem equals my arrogance.'

Put another way: the inconvenient truth about Kanye's criticism is that though it may be in bad taste, his taste isn't bad. Looking back a decade later, it *is* absurd that Gretchen Wilson won the Best New Artist AMA over Kanye, whose *The College Dropout* is a debut that ranks among hip hop's very best, the peer of *Ready to Die*, *Illmatic* and *Reasonable Doubt*. Where—who—is Gretchen Wilson? Though it may have frazzled some producers at NBC, and hurt George Bush's feelings, Kanye's comments about the federal government's response to Katrina anticipated Black Lives Matter, and the vital, uncomfortable questions it raised about the prejudices of people and institutions that don't consider themselves racist, but are. And I'mma let you finish, but let's be honest: though she'd later go on to write a record to rival any by Bruce Springsteen, *1989*, Taylor Swift's 'You Belong to Me' doesn't hold a candle to Beyoncé's 'Single Ladies'. The moment Kanye rose to register his complaint wasn't just painful live television; it was also the finest impromptu review of our time.

But Kanye's career as a pre-Aristotelian critic coincided with the rise of Poptimism, which usurped the alt-weekly, record-store snobbery of the 1990s with a catholicity of enthusiasms. A love for confected pop and chanteuse pabulum became the new mark of refinement; only taste itself was gauche. *Gawker's* Tom Scocca called the competing attitudes snark (think Dorothy Parker) and smarm (think your kindergarten teacher). But even in the decade when smarm had roundly won the battle over snark, Kanye had the trait common to all critics: he just couldn't help himself. In a time when we lived by Thumper's Law, Kanye's critiques struck anywhere. About the music that made him famous he said: 'I don't even listen to rap.

My apartment is too nice to listen to rap in.' He tried his hand at literary criticism, siding with Larkin ('books are a load of crap') and Berryman ('literature bores me, especially great literature'): 'Sometimes people write novels and they just be so wordy and self-absorbed. I am not a fan of books.' He even took a hard line on H2O: 'I hate when I'm on a flight and I wake up with a water bottle next to me like oh great now I gotta be responsible for this water bottle.'

In 2015, Kanye was ahead of his time, and behind it. The baby was early, and the album—*Swish*, the overdue follow-up to *Yeezus*—was late. The world will have to be tided over by the remarkable speech he delivered in September when accepting the MTV VMA Vanguard Award. After Taylor Swift herself handed him his moon man, he said: 'I been conflicted bro. I just wanted people to like me more. But fuck that bro.' What followed was a robust defence of his public outbursts. 'I didn't know how to say the right thing, the perfect thing,' he said. 'Sometimes I feel like I died for the artist's opinion. For artists to be able to have an opinion.' (Also, obviously: 'Y'all might be thinking right now, "I wonder did he smoke something before he came out here?" And the answer is yes, I rolled up a little something, I knocked the edge off.') In other words, he was given the prize as an artist, but he accepted it as a critic.

IV

THE SHOCK ABSORBER

There is a circle and there is a line.

I'm in the line, queued in a posh Toronto neighbourhood between the man who just lost the race to be prime minister, and the country's most powerful newspaper magnate. In line with us are writers, journalists, socialites, industrialists, all wending their way through the warm June evening to be received by Scott Griffin, the redoubtable patron, founder and host of one of the world's richest literary awards, the Griffin Poetry Prize. Tonight is the annual awards gala, an opulent celebration of the written word at which Mr Griffin will award two writers $65,000 each for having authored a book.

Raif Badawi is in the circle. It surrounds him after Friday prayers at the al-Jafali mosque in Jeddah, Saudi Arabia. Soldiers have unloaded Badawi from a bus, then marched him in shackles through the square as a crowd encircles him. By order of a Saudi court, he will now be flogged with a cane. An eyewitness will later tell Amnesty International: 'Passers-by joined them and the crowd grew. But no one knew why Raif was about to be punished. Is he a killer, they asked? A criminal?'

He is a writer. In 2010, he founded a website called *Free Saudi Liberals*, where he briefly agitated for free speech, the separation of church and state, liberalism, feminism, and solidarity with his fellow free thinkers. 'As soon as a thinker starts to reveal his ideas,' he wrote in August 2010, 'you will find hundreds of fatwas that accuse him of being an infidel just because he had the courage to discuss some sacred topics.' Before long, he attracted the attention of his authoritarian state and by 2012, he had been arrested, and charged with apostasy, which carries a mandatory death sentence. His Wahabi Sharia judge was lenient, and in 2013 sentenced Badawi to six years in a Saudi prison, and six hundred lashes. When Badawi appealed the sentence, the judge increased his punishment to ten years in prison, and a thousand lashes, which are administered fifty at a time to the writer's bare back on Friday afternoons.

The eyewitness told Amnesty International what happened next. A man in uniform emerged from the circle holding a large cane and ordered Badawi to kneel. He raised the cane and for an instant it is stood straight as a radius before wailing through the air and bouncing off Badawi's back. Raif raised his head and closed his eyes. The man in the uniform counted: one. Badawi's wife and three daughters have fled Saudi Arabia, and live now as political refugees in the kind of country Badawi has argued Saudi Arabia could become: Canada. Two. In one of his final essays on *Free Saudi Liberals*, he quoted Albert Camus, a writer everyone in the line for the Griffin Prize gala probably knows: 'The only way to deal with an unfree world is to become so absolutely free that your very existence is an act of rebellion.' Three. When the man in the uniform has counted to fifty, Badawi is dragged back to the bus. For nineteen more Fridays, he will return to the circle.

The circle and the line can never meet. Like the wheel of a car and its flat undercarriage, a shock absorber separates them.

Scott Griffin produces that shock absorber. His company, General Kinetics of Brampton, Ontario, has a subcontract on the largest foreign trade deal in Canadian history. It is an arms deal—one that appears to violate our own export regulations—negotiated by the Harper government on behalf of London, Ontario's General Dynamics Land Systems, for the delivery of $15 billion worth of light armoured vehicles. A kind of tank on wheels, LAVs are one of the most formidable fighting machines ever conceived by the human mind. The purchaser is the Kingdom of Saudi Arabia, Raif Badawi's jailor and torturer. For every single Light Armoured Vehicle the Saudis are buying, Mr Griffin's General Kinetics is providing the shock absorbers.

In June of 2012 Raif Badawi was arrested and I went to the Griffin Prize gala. He and I were twenty-nine. But because I was born in Canada and Mr Badawi was born in Saudi Arabia, our convictions, however similar, have had diametric consequences on our lives. According to the *Economist's* Democracy Index for that year, I lived in the eighth freest country in the world and Badawi lived in the eighth least free, barely ahead of Equatorial Guinea, Turkmenistan, Chad and North Korea. Badawi risked his life for his writing, while I made a living from mine.

That year, I was working as the poetry editor of *The Walrus* and as the poetry columnist for the *National Post*, both Canadian institutions with well-read and well-heeled audiences. And so for a few years, every June I was invited to the Griffin festivities. Before the Griffin Prize, Canadian poetry was precisely as luxurious, and as lucrative, as you're imagining—that is to say, not at all. Some poets are lucky enough to be tenured professors at universities, but most carve out precarious livings doing whatever will pay the bills between visits from the muse.

Modest but crucial government subsidies to poets and publishers help buttress an art form for which there's virtually no market demand or public interest. Books appear in print runs of five hundred copies, receive maybe a short review in one of the country's mostly unread literary journals, then promptly recede into oblivion. A couple books each year are singled out, from the hundreds published, for one of the handful of prizes available to poets, the purses of which vary from the decoder ring awarded to winners of the ReLit Prize—a piece of jewellery which I imagine is even hard to pawn—to the $20,000 offered by the long-toothed and increasingly out-of-touch Governor General's Award.

At least, that was as good as it got until Scott Griffin swooped in. Founded in 2001, the Griffin Prize was unlike anything the Canadian poetry world had ever seen, a beast as rare and regal as its namesake, the Griffin, a half lion, half eagle that shuttled Dante and Beatrice into Paradise, and guarded the treasures of the ancient Middle East. It registered with the Canada Revenue Agency as a private charitable foundation with a $2.5 million endowment. Its founding trustees were a roll call of literary luminaires: Canadians Margaret Atwood, Michael Ondaatje and the playwright David Young; American poet Robert Haas; Britain's Robin Robertson. The chairman of the trust is Scott Griffin, whose 'occupation or line of business' was recorded in CRA filings simply as 'entrepreneur'.

In its first year, the Griffin Prize awarded $40,000 each to a winning Canadian and foreign poet. Today the Trust's assets stand at $9,009,077, and each year it doles out two prizes of $65,000. The shortlist of three Canadians and four foreigners gives a public reading on a scale not seen since T.S. Eliot and Allen Ginsberg filled football stadiums in the 1940s, with thousands of Torontonians packing into tony Koerner Hall. Every poet on the shortlist is paid $10,000 as a 'reading fee'.

But the real glitz is saved for the evening after the readings, the night of the gala, where the winners are anointed as Scott Griffin produces their cheques, and shines his solar spotlight on an art form better acquainted with the shade. Three hundred and sixty three days a year, poetry plays next to no role at all in our cultural life, and W.H. Auden is right when he sighs, in his elegy to W.B. Yeats: 'Poetry makes nothing happen.' Once a year though, on the night of the Griffin gala, Auden is wrong.

The first time I stood in the gala's receiving line, I was sandwiched between Michael Ignatieff, fresh off his federal election loss, and Conrad Black, fresh out of prison. As a Canadian poet, I was nonetheless a thorn between two roses. The gala is held in Toronto's historic Distillery District, once home to the world's largest distiller, Godderham and Worts, and now a sequestered playpen for downtown's upwardly mobile. Entering the exquisite old distillery, I found the scale and opulence of the event intoxicating. Dozens of tables were appointed with vaulting floral arrangements. A legion of servers zigzagged slinging canapés. Past me walked former Governor General Adrienne Clarkson. Over there was the actor and director Sarah Polley. After dinner—which is so good it hampers conversation—I left my fiancée to go to the washroom and returned to find a strange man with his arm around her chair. It's Jian Ghomeshi.

The Griffin Prize, more than anything, is a validation of the vanity of poets, the poorest and most ignored of artists, who on one night a year can attenuate their self-loathing just enough to indulge their self-regard, and believe without reservation that we are, as Percy Bysshe Shelley called us, the 'unacknowledged legislators of the world'. Inebriating as it was, I had to leave the 2012 gala early. The Griffin Trust had arranged for me to meet one of my heroes the next morning, the Nobel Prize–winning Irish poet Seamus Heaney. They had flown Heaney in to award him the Griffin Lifetime Achievement Award, and asked me if I'd like to interview him. In the end, we would talk for an hour. He would tell me stories about Robert Lowell and teaching at Harvard, and would sign my weathered copy of his *Collected Poems*. A year later he was dead. If it weren't for Mr Griffin's largesse, I would never have met him.

The night of the gala, I lay awake, thrilled, intimidated and a little drunk, running through Heaney's poems in my head. In

'Chekhov on Sakhalin', he imagines the Russian writer destroying a glass of expensive cognac the night he arrives at a penal colony: 'When he staggered up and smashed it on the stones/It rang as clearly as the convicts' chains/That haunted him.' A few days later in Saudi Arabia, a writer I'd never heard of, Raif Badawi, would be in shackles. Drifting off, I imagined the damage my poet friends were probably still doing to Mr Griffin's pocketbook by way of that open bar. Then for the first time, I wondered: How *did* Scott Griffin make all that money?

———————

Silver-haired, a trim and handsome seventy-seven, in a double-breasted navy blazer that can only be described as nautical, Scott Griffin takes the stage looking like Blue Rodeo's Jim Cuddy dressed up as The Millionaire from *Gilligan's Island*. He's on YouTube, giving a TED Talk entitled 'Why Poetry'. 'Poetry is the essence of language,' he intones gravely, 'and language is the mirror of the soul.' Okay, so as a literary critic, he's no Dr Johnson. Still, one can't help but be convinced, over the fifteen minutes of his lecture, that poetry is fundamental to Scott Griffin.

'When we were growing up as kids,' he says of his childhood in Hamilton, Ontario, 'my father used to read to us in the evenings. And a lot of it was poetry.' His father seems to have been a well-read man, a cultured disciplinarian whose taste in verse ended where Modernism began, with Ezra Pound and T. S. Eliot. One night, Scott Griffin recited 'it really must be Nice', by e.e. cummings, a slight lyric about juggling a shitty job and the quotidian humiliations of family life. His father was impressed. 'With the recitation of that poem,' Mr Griffin says, 'I'd grown up, and he recognized it.'

Later, after attending a boarding school that, in his TED Talk, he calls 'a beat 'em up, keep 'em cold kind of place', Mr

Griffin took a degree in English and Philosophy at Bishop's University in Lennoxville, Que (where he would later become Chancellor). There, he encountered a transformative professor, Arthur Motyer, a Rhodes Scholar whose ability to reel off entire Dylan Thomas poems by heart made an indelible impression upon the young man.

Then he graduated. In our interview, Mr Griffin told me: 'My father basically said, "Your free life is over and now you've got to go and work." In those days, you took the first thing that came along, and I worked for BP—British Petroleum—for about ten or twelve years'. Soon Mr Griffin realized that his true calling was the high-stakes world of venture capital. 'I recognized there was more money chasing fewer deals,' he told me, and so in 1981, he 'formed a manufacturing company in the automotive industry, and it got pretty big.' That company was Meridian Technologies, a magnesium die-casting concern originally based in Strathroy, Ontario, which by the mid-1990s employed two thousand people and banked, according to Mr Griffin, about $175 million in annual sales.

But as he writes in his memoir *My Heart Is Africa: A Flying Adventure*, by 1995 Meridian Technologies, a publicly traded company, 'had grown in size and prospects with two large international shareholders struggling to gain control. This eventually led to a boardroom tussle, which I lost.' Mr Griffin calls what befell him after the ouster a midlife crisis.

'For years,' writes Mr Griffin, 'I had dreamed of breaking away from business into something completely different—combining adventure with an altruistic pursuit in an underdeveloped country'. That underdeveloped country wasn't Canadian poetry; it was Kenya. 'I had always been intrigued by the idea of Africa,' he writes. 'Africa conjured up all that was fundamental, raw, and powerful, with a deep undercurrent of mystery. The heavy beat of dark African nights suggested incarnate desire, danger, and fear.'

Casting around for an NGO that could use him, Mr Griffin discovered the African Medical and Research Foundation, which ran something called the Flying Doctors Service of East Africa, a rag-tag air ambulance outfit that flew bush planes into remote communities—nearly always under dangerous conditions—to administer medical aid. He signed on as a consultant, on a two-year unpaid term beginning in 1995, to turn around the faltering and mismanaged Flying Doctors Service.

With the altruism part battened down, Mr Griffin turned to arranging the adventure, beginning with his mode of transportation: his own private plane, a single-engine Cessna, which he would fly solo from Canada to Africa, an almost pathologically dangerous decision (that, it must be admitted, makes for a gripping yarn): 'A navigational miscalculation, an operational error or misjudgement from this point forward could lead to fuel exhaustion, mechanical failure, or loss of direction, forcing me to ditch into a fearsome sea.'

In *My Heart Is Africa*, when he isn't consulting for the Flying Doctors Service, ever the adventuring venture capitalist, Mr Griffin can be found running hard bargains at high stakes, the consequences of which can spiral into unforeseen disasters. On Christmas Day, 1995, a teenaged Samburu warrior wanders into the resort where the Griffins are laying over on a leg of their aerial safari. The boy offers to sell Scott his own hunting spear, an heirloom he'd inherited, with which he and his family had killed five lions over two generations. Mr Griffin, who thought that the boy's asking price of a thousand shillings—or two Canadian dollars—was too steep, makes a counter offer: a short sunset flight in his plane in exchange for the spear. Mr Griffin, his infinitely patient wife, Krystyne, and the Samburu boy all cram into the Cessna, take off, and shortly thereafter crash on Lake Turkana's South Island, a volcanic outcropping inhabited only by the crocodiles that sun themselves on its shores.

A group of Turkana fishermen—the Samburu clan's mortal enemies—come to their aid, and after some tense negotiations, they all eat freshly caught tilapia together for Christmas dinner. The following morning, they are rescued by a major in the Kenyan army, who lands his attack helicopter on the South Island moonscape and returns Mr Griffin, his wife, and the Samburu boy back to the resort. Twelve minutes after dropping them off, the major's helicopter is shot down by Turkana rebels. Everyone on board is killed, and a minor civil war between the Turkana and the Kenyan Army ensues. None other than Margaret Atwood calls Mr Griffin, on his book cover, 'one of the great romantics'.

'It was on those long solo flights,' he tells his audience at the TED Talk, 'that I rediscovered the joy of reciting poetry.' Around the same time, he discovered the money to be made in manufacturing arms components. In 1996, Mr Griffin took possession of General Kinetics and within a few short years had parlayed his lifelong love of poetry into a daring charitable intervention. I asked him why, and he said: 'You know I did end up making some money; and then what are you going to do with it? We tend to support and get interested in our interests, one of which was English literature.'

And he didn't stop with his eponymous prize; in 2002, he rescued the House of Anansi, a storied Canadian press (and the publisher of my first book) from Jack Stoddart's haemorrhaging General Publishing company, which was $45 million in debt. He purchased Anansi during bankruptcy protection for $400,000, about the cost of a small Toronto condo, in cash. Margaret Atwood hailed him 'a culture hero'.

Mr Griffin ends his TED Talk with a poem. From memory,

he recites Matthew Arnold's 'Dover Beach', a meditation on 'the turbid ebb and flow/of human misery'. His delivery is studied, but there's an unnerving dissonance between the sureness of Mr Griffin's performance and Arnold's fearful ambivalence:

> And we are here as on a darkling plain
> Swept with confused alarms of struggle and flight,
> Where ignorant armies clash by night.

———————

Ed Fast had a very good Valentine's Day. On February 14th, 2014, Canada's Minister for International Trade stood on the production floor of the world's fourth-largest defence firm, London, Ontario's own General Dynamics Land Systems and announced the biggest foreign trade deal in Canadian history, The Armoured Brigades Program. Brokered by the Canadian Commercial Corporation, a crown outfit that negotiates with foreign buyers on behalf of Canadian exporters, the fourteen-year contract would be worth $15 billion. And every cent of that windfall would be spent on a single Canadian weapon of war, the Light Armoured Vehicle, and by a single foreign purchaser, the Kingdom of Saudi Arabia.

The LAV is a multi-generational family of military vehicles manufactured at General Dynamics' (also known as GDLS) London plant. In its most common configuration, it is an eight-wheeled fighting vehicle that looks like a small tank with wheels instead of tracks. 'Small', in this case, means weighing close to twenty tonnes. It can travel the distance between Toronto and Montreal—roughly 600 kilometres—at 100 km/h without refuelling. Operated by a crew of three, it can ferry up to seven additional soldiers as passengers, who on command will pour out of the LAV and onto the battlefield.

Any enemy unfortunate enough to be on the business end of a LAV will likely suffer the fate of the Light Brigade, 'theirs but to do and die'. Armed with a 25-milimetre, 300-pound chain gun with a range of three kilometres, there isn't much a modern LAV can't destroy: airplanes and helicopters, other LAVs and of course people. It has the aura of some terrible, resilient insect, its many antennae rocking stiffly and synchronized as the whole vehicle recoils into its shock absorbers after it fires. With half of its wheels destroyed, it can still roar deliberately downrange. It has two secondary machine guns for use against personnel, as well as four grenade launchers embedded in its chassis. Its main gun can be replaced with weapons systems that range from a tank cannon to a mortar system capable of firing cluster bombs. Fully amphibious, it has rear propellers that allow it to ford any inland body of water. LAVs can even be parachuted into theatres of war from a C-130 Hercules.

An earlier iteration of the vehicle, the LAV-25, saw action in 1989's Operation Just Cause, when the United States invaded Panama ostensibly to oust its increasingly erratic dictator General Manuel Noriega, but also to keep its canal, which joins the Atlantic and Pacific Oceans, in the hands of a regime friendly to American interests. They were deployed in the first Persian Gulf War, when oil-rich Iraq's Saddam Hussein invaded Kuwait and found himself on the wrong side of George H. W. Bush's moral indignation. The Canadian military bought a few LAV-25s, christening them with the decidedly parochial field name 'Bison' before sending them on our peacekeeping mission in Bosnia in 1992.

But by the mid-1990s, both the American and Canadian militaries were recognizing the need for a more comprehensive update of the armoured personnel carrier. Working with both countries' departments of defence, General Dynamics was awarded contracts to design and build the next generation of LAVs. The Canadian Army ordered a total of 651 LAV-IIIs; the Americans ordered 4,466 Strykers, variations on the same vehicle.

Ever since, LAVs have been big business for General Dynamics and the more than 500 Canadian subcontractors in its supply chain whose individual contributions are combined by General Dynamics to form the colossal fighting machine. Until recently, the United States was by far the biggest customer. But also lining up to buy the LAV have been Australia, New Zealand and Colombia.

And, most controversially, Saudi Arabia. As far back as 1992, the same year the Americans were forcing their way through the Iraqi desert, General Dynamics, with the help of the Canadian Commercial Corporation, minted its first arms deal with the Saudis, an order for 1,600 LAVs to be delivered over the next decade.

That contract was an order of magnitude smaller than the enormous one proudly unveiled by Minister Fast this past February [2014]. Still, something made it very troubling indeed: the outfit writing the cheque to General Dynamics that year was none other than the Saudi Arabia National Guard. The SANG, as it's known in military circles, is not the Saudi Arabian Army, whose job is to defend the country from external threats. The SANG is larger than the Saudi Army. It's not even overseen by the Saudi Ministry of Defence. It is headed by Mutaib bin Abdullah, the son of King Abdullah, the country's former autocratic ruler who died just a month before Minister Fast made his chest-thumping announcement on that factory floor in Southwestern Ontario. The SANG's 125,000 soldiers are mostly Bedouin tribesman and Wahhabis loyal to the ruling family. (Until 1954, the SANG was called the Office of Jihad and Mujahidin.) And they have a single purpose: to act as a kind of mass personal bodyguard for the despotic house of Saud, defending the royal family from any and all internal threats.

Threats like, say, the ideas of writers like Raif Badawi.

The SANG is one of the key reasons there was not, and never will be, an Arab Spring in Saudi Arabia—or, for that matter, in neighbouring Bahrain. In 2011, the SANG made a rare sortie beyond the borders of Saudi Arabia, when the King of Bahrain, another Sunni autocrat, asked for help in dispersing the largely Shiite protesters who had taken to the streets to agitate for democracy. According to a report at the time from the Washington Institute for Near East Policy, 'the Saudi forces arriving on the island are said to number 1,000, along with about 150 vehicles, including wheeled, light-armoured vehicles with roof-mounted heavy machine guns.' Those were Canadian-made LAVs.

For a month in 2011, thousands of pro-democracy protesters had been camped out in the Pearl Roundabout, the central square of Manama, Bahrain's capital. After the Saudi forces crossed the King Fahd Causeway into Bahrain, the country's autocratic government declared a curfew, which came into force at four in the afternoon on March 16. An hour later, security forces, reinforced by armoured vehicles, tanks and helicopters, encircled the protesters and opened fire from all sides. Eight protesters were killed that night, hundreds were injured, and more than a thousand were arrested. By five o'clock, the Arab Spring in Bahrain was over.

Until this past year, and besides the 1992 Saudi contract, LAV sales have conformed to the Department of Foreign Affairs' prohibition of the sale of arms to countries 'whose governments have a persistent record of serious violations of the human rights of their citizens', or if there is a 'reasonable risk that the goods might be used against the civilian population'.

But the tragedy of the arms dealer is that he can only sell to the good guys so long as they're buying. As the wars in Iraq and Afghanistan wound down, a precipice approached. The 2013–2014 CCC report warns: 'Sales in support of the U.S. military have been $700 million or more annually for the last several years.... However, CCC anticipates sales to the U.S. DoD to decrease to amounts which are well below traditional levels in the range of $550 million per year, given the significant decline in U.S. DoD spending.' In that same report, the CCC massively underplays how life-saving last February's Saudi LAV deal is to General Dynamics, its 500 sub-contractors, and even the CCC itself. Despite the American downsizing noted in the report, 'with strategic focus on key geographies and Canadian capabilities, CCC and Canadian exporters enjoyed significant success in 2013-2014, culminating in the signing of the historic multi-billion-dollar Armoured Brigades contract.'

How many LAVs are the Saudis buying? The government isn't saying. But according to Forecast International, LAVs cost, on average, about a million dollars each. So $15 billion could buy as many as 15,000 LAVs, more than three times the number that the American military has ever purchased. In fact, despite the fact that Minister Fast proudly gasconaded about the deal when it was announced, the Harper government has otherwise remained stubbornly tight-lipped about its specifics—like which divisions of the Saudi armed forces will be piloting the killing machines—breaking its silence only to trumpet that it's good news for our economy. Both the CCC report and Minister Fast himself have boasted that the Armoured Brigades Program is sustaining or creating more than 3,000 jobs—14 percent of those in Southern Ontario—over the next 14 years.

What remains to be addressed is how the Armoured Brigades Program meets the safeguards of our export standards. Saudi Arabia has one of the worst human rights records on earth, and has deployed LAVs against civilian populations to crush democratic protests. Women are not only not allowed to vote in the hereditary kingdom's rigidly proscribed and mostly symbolic elections; they're not allowed to drive. Its civil society is based on a strict Wahhabi interpretation of Sharia law. Thieves can have their hands amputated as official state punishment. Drug use and adultery earn death sentences, which have been carried out by crucifixion.

And it's only getting worse. The kingdom is on track this year to a perform a record number of beheadings, 85 so far, which Saudi officials say demonstrate their commitment to 'maintaining security and realizing justice'.

Speaking of justice, in 2007, a woman known as Qatif Girl (after her hometown) sought Saudi's version of it after she was abducted and gang raped by a former boyfriend and six of his buddies. But because she had been conveyed to the location of her assault in a car by a man who wasn't her husband or blood relative, she was found to have been in a state of *khalwa*—being alone with an unrelated man—and was sentenced to 90 lashes as punishment. When she told her story to the media, she earned 200 more, and the lawyer who represented her, known for taking on contentious cases, had his license revoked.

And then there's Raif Badawi, a writer who for the crime of eloquently agitating for the same intellectual and political liberties which are every Canadian's inheritance—the rule of law, liberalism, free expression—is being imprisoned and tortured by the very government we're enriching ourselves by arming.

Outraged with how religion poisoned the lives of Saudi Arabians, he wrote in 2010:

'Secularism … is the practical solution to lift countries (including ours) out of the third world and into the first world. States based on religious ideology … have nothing except the fear of God and an inability to face up to life. Look at what happened after the European peoples succeeded in removing the clergy from public life and restricting them to their churches. They built up human beings and promoted enlightenment, creativity and rebellion. States which are based on religion confine their people in the circle of faith and fear.'

The Canadian literary world, it turns out, is now intimately connected to the Armour Brigades Program, the largest—and maybe most heinous—foreign trade deal in our country's history. It takes thirty seconds online to discover how. Go to the Griffin Prize website. Click on the About page. There you'll find glowing biographies for all of the Foundation's trustees.

The award's eponymous founder comes first. It begins: 'Scott Griffin is the Chairman, Director and controlling shareholder of General Kinetics Engineering Corp.' Google 'General Kinetics'. You'll discover that it is a Brampton company that makes shock absorbers for military vehicles. 'GK has served the military market for over 25 years,' reads the company's own website, adding that it supplies 'all of the U.S. Army's telescopic shock absorbers for tracked vehicles, and a large portion of those for wheeled vehicles.' It goes on: 'with the introduction of Hydropneumatic Suspensions in the mid-90's, GK became a supplier to GDLS [General Dynamics] and earned "Medallion of Success" honors … for its work on the Stryker program.' On its Industry Canada webpage, meanwhile, General Kinetics is described as having 'produced all the suspensions on LAV III'.

I recently spoke to Mr Griffin by phone as he was transiting the Panama Canal in his sailboat, a waterway that LAVs played no small part in keeping open to Western seafaring. When I asked him if General Kinetics had a subcontract on the $15 billion Saudi LAV deal, he paused for a second—a seagull cried into his silence—then he answered: 'We're supplying General Dynamics with the shock absorbers.'

———————

Ezra Pound called writers 'the antennae of the race'. More often than not our Spidey sense is scanning the air for even the subtlest of ethical lapses. So I began asking poets, writers, journalists, professors and editors—the people you find in line for the Griffin Prize gala—the question I asked Scott Griffin himself: Is there a contradiction in the fact that Mr Griffin has dedicated a good deal of his time, fortune and energy to supporting writers, while simultaneously supplying weapons parts to a regime that destroys them? Mr Griffin himself said: 'Well it's a good question,' then went on, 'I don't see it personally as a conflict, but I see how somebody might think it is.'

Somebody: singular. It's not quite that few. But my question sends the vast majority of the free-thinking liberals I've asked into equivocating tailspins, rhetorical reverses and magical thinking. An esteemed literary editor told me he thought Scott Griffin was a saint, even after I'd explained what General Kinetics makes. A professor at a prestigious American journalism school couldn't see what the big deal was; when I asked if it was because shock absorbers weren't 'weapon-y' enough, he agreed. Too many people to count, including a former winner of the Griffin Prize, have argued that being entangled at all in the contradictions of capitalism precludes me from interrogating this particular incongruity. After all, I used to work for *The Walrus*.

which runs ads by Enbridge; I worked on this story at the Banff Centre, which is supported by energy companies; I on occasion wear jeans made in China.

Many others have confessed that as a Canadian poet—starving for both cash and attention—they can't afford to even consider whether supporting the prize, at the expense of like-minded liberal dissidents, may be morally compromising to our literary community, and to our souls.

Eventually, I asked the one Canadian writer who can be counted on for clear moral thinking: Margaret Atwood. I sent her an e-mail noting that Mr Griffin's General Kinetics has a subcontract on the colossal Saudi-LAV deal, and asked what she thought it meant for Canadian writers who support the Griffin Prize. I asked Ms Atwood in part because I'd seen her repeatedly tweet about the plight of Raif Badawi while also being a Trustee Emeritus of the Griffin Prize. Ms Atwood was also on a boat—presumably a different boat than Mr Griffin—and had to wait a few days before responding. She eventually wrote back through her assistant, annotating my questions in a bright red font that, towards the end, she also highlights yellow.

When I asked her if there was a contradiction at the heart of the Griffin Prize, she wrote: 'I think it's a Sophie's Choice. On the one hand, conduct the business like a business, i.e. any dollar is the same as any other dollar. On the other hand, refuse to sell to some while selling to others, and lose all the business.' It may very well be the case that General Kinetics cannot afford to turn down the subcontract on the Saudi deal, though I can't be as sure as Ms Atwood. It's only a Sophie's Choice though if the capitalist's two children are his pocketbook and his conscience, and I have a feeling which is more likely to be sent on the gloomier walk.

Under my note about our mutual concern for Raif Badawi, and liberal writers like him in the wake of the $15 billion Saudi LAV deal, she interjected: 'The Saudi regime could persecute Mr Badawi with a piece of string. I don't think those weapons are instrumental in such cases.' Here again, I can't share Ms Atwood's certainty. In my research, I haven't been able to definitively confirm which departments of the Saudi military or security forces will be outfitted with LAVs from the Armoured Brigades Program, though the enormity of the order suggests that the Saudis could be outfitting a great number of their security branches, including the Committee for the Promotion of Virtue and Prevention of Vice, which is in all likeliness the organization that executed the arrest of Raif Badawi. The Harper government's refusal to discuss the sale is making any certainty on the matter—including Ms Atwood's—profoundly irresponsible. We do know though that the LAVs Canada sold to the Saudis in the 1990s were used for crushing liberal dissent, when they invaded Bahrain to brutally end its Arab Spring in 2011.

'They are instrumental, ie. in maybe keeping SA out of the hands of ISIS,' Ms Atwood argued. There has been a great deal of speculation in the intelligence community that, although ISIS has blustered on social media that one of its eventual targets is the House of Saud, ISIS, essentially a marauding Sunni militia, is in fact also receiving a substantial portion of its funding from Saudi Arabia. Sir Richard Dearlove, the former head of Britain's MI6 intelligence agency, told *The Independent* that he's certain a great deal of ISIS's financial support is coming from Saudi Arabia. A leaked, classified Pentagon brief calls Saudi Arabia its region's 'kernel of evil', warning that it is 'active at every level of the terrorist chain'. In a 2009 cable released by Wikileaks, then Secretary of State Hillary Clinton warned: 'Saudi Arabia remains a critical financial support base for Al-Qa'ida, the Taliban … and other terrorist groups.' Fifteen of the nineteen 9/11 hijackers were Saudi. So was Osama bin Laden.

'Is it the weapons,' Ms Atwood asks, 'or is it the ill of those directing them?' That rang a bell. It's the National Rifle Association bumper sticker, rephrased: Guns don't kill people. People kill people.

When I asked whether or not she knew of Mr Griffin's ownership of General Kinetics when she joined the Griffin Trust board, she said no. She withdrew from the board in 2014 and became a 'trustee emeritus' the same year as the Armoured Brigades Program was announced, so I asked whether or not the two had anything to do with one another. She responded: 'I am no longer on the board, and was not on it when this sale was announced.' She added: 'I do not wish to be used as a stick to beat Scott Griffin.'

This is where the highlighting starts, as she begins to mount a robust defence of the arms industry. 'Are all arms manufactures (sic) bad?' she asks. 'If the Allies had had no arm (sic) in WW2, Hitle (sic) would have won. Would that have been good?' For what it's worth, it doesn't particularly bother me that General Kinetics makes shock absorbers for LAVs that are sold to the Canadian Forces. I don't even really mind that they end up in the U.S. Stryker. I part company with General Kinetics on the Saudi deal.

That said, most of the writers I know begin to froth at the mouth at the very word 'military', never mind 'American military'. Scott Griffin himself said to me: 'A lot of the literary world is probably anti the army or the navy or the air force, but you know suddenly you need them and they're very pro.' He's calling us duplicitous, but ours is a different sort of duplicity, one that actually works in Mr Griffin's favour; with it, he can get Margaret Atwood to defend his involvement in a Saudi arms deal by invoking Hitler.

'There are no simple answers,' Ms Atwood argues, 'when it's a choice of evils. One should try to choose the lesser evil, but how do you know you're right?' Canadian writers, like almost all human beings, ground their morality in a rational self-interest, and the truth is that we can't afford to question the Griffin Prize or the business decisions of its patron. As Ed Fast said of the Armoured Brigades Program, the Griffin Prize is too good for our economy—or so the conventional wisdom goes.

Ms Atwood warned me: 'Perhaps you should examine your own motives a little more closely here. I've seen a lot of take-downs in my life, and some failed attempts.' I think she's suggesting that I may have sour grapes about having not won the Griffin Prize myself. She continues: 'If … you want to kick poetry in the slats at a time when the humanities and the arts in general are under fire from the very same people who made the Saudi deal possible, then full steam ahead. Jump up and down on Scott Griffin. Harper will applaud your efforts.'

I don't want to kick poetry in the slats any more than Margaret Atwood does. I too have dedicated my life to it.

But the Griffin Prize less supports poetry than a handful of poets. Like the Flying Doctors Service, the Griffin Prize isn't really a macro-solution to poetry's marginality, but a single, daring, high-stakes intervention that changes one life at a time, one night a year. It has been around for 15 years, almost a generation. Fourteen people have won it, out of the 500 or so published, living Canadian poets. Why 14 and not 15? Because Anne Carson, the most famous Canadian poet alive, has won it twice. She's also been shortlisted for it twice, along with Erin Moure, Dionne Brand, P.K. Page, Ken Babstock, David McFadden and

Phil Hall. Don McKay has been shortlisted three times, as has Erin Moure, who has also served as a judge. Suzanne Buffam served as a judge two years after being shortlisted. In 2014 Robert Bringhurst was a judge, 13 years after he was shortlisted and two years after his wife, Jan Zwicky, was shortlisted. Karen Solie, who was shortlisted in 2002, was a judge in 2007, won in 2010, and is now a trustee. Are these the only poets writing good books? By no stretch of the imagination. And yet still writers are afraid to criticize the prize, even as the fact that its founder manufactures weapons parts is freely available on the prize's own website, and even when informed by a journalist that those weapons are arming a regime that would happily torture them too, if only they'd had the misfortune of being born in Saudi Arabia, like Raif Badawi.

———————

'Does a wrong cancel a right?' Ms Atwood asked me. 'Would seem to be the core question.' Powerful people have been giving writers prizes and patronage for a very long time, but it isn't until the twentieth century, with the founding of the Nobel Prize, that the benefits to the benefactor become obvious. Alfred Nobel invented dynamite, from which he made his substantial fortune. In 1888, Alfred's brother Ludwig died in the French city of Cannes. French newspapers reported his death but confused him with Alfred, and published his obituary under the headline 'Le marchand de la mort est mort.' The merchant of death is dead. Alfred Nobel had the unenviable experience of reading his own obituary, and it wasn't pretty. But after having made a killing from death, how do you change your obit from a pan to a rave? He needed a right to cancel his wrongs, as Ms Atwood puts it. Nobel quietly amended his will so that upon his death the vast majority of his fortune was commuted to a trust that would disburse prizes, named in his own honour, for humanity's greatest achievements in five categories—Chemistry, Peace, Medicine, Physics and Literature. With the stroke of a pen, Nobel became noble.

James F. English, in his book *The Economy of Prestige*, calls this 'cultural laundering'. Joseph Pulitzer isn't remembered for the sensational, gossipy, ambulance-chasing 'yellow journalism' he helped pioneer at his paper the *New York World*; with the creation of the Pulitzer Prize, his name is now synonymous with his profession's Platonic Ideal. Jay Pritzker, English argues, made one of America's great fortunes by propagating his aesthetically unremarkable Hyatt hotels around the world, then founded the Pritzker prize for architectural achievement. Peter Munk, the chairman and founder of Barrick Gold, the world's largest gold mining company, may very well be remembered as the kindly old man with the Hungarian accent who brought Tony Blair and a dying Christopher Hitchens to Toronto to chat about religion for the Munk Debates.

The Griffin Prize itself, in other words, is a shock absorber—intended or not—for its own, and its founder's, reputations. As its patron travels over increasingly dodgy terrain, he can remain upright because his country's most esteemed literati can equivocate themselves into coils. Ms Atwood wrote through her assistant: 'I am quite puzzled by his questions, as they come out of left field. It's like saying should one go to the library funded by Andrew Carnegie because the latter was bad to unions, etc. Or should he be going to the Banff Centre considering the lethal effects of the oil industry, etc.' Even the mere inquiry, by a journalist and poet, into the contradictions of the Griffin Prize is a category error, and this from Margaret Atwood, who in March tweeted to Rob Nicholson, the Minister of Foreign Affairs, petitioning him to do what he can to help Raif Badawi.

That would be the same Rob Nicholson whose own ministry's export regulations clearly prohibit arms sales to the Saudis, guidelines which were established so that as a country we can avoid implicating ourselves in atrocities like the one that has befallen Badawi.

'Pushing armaments for megaprofits,' Ms Atwood wrote, 'when it is not a case of (for instance) an involvement of one's own country in a war is no doubt reprehensible.' As far as I can tell, she's speaking theoretically, and not specifically, having just mounted a defence of Mr Griffin's involvement in the Armoured Brigades Program. She goes on: 'If you want to nail somebody for dealing with the Saudis or allowing such dealings or fostering such dealings, I think you've got the wrong vampire. You should be examining the role of the government.'

Here is the essence of the national tragedy that is the Armoured Brigades Program, which we can glimpse through the narrow, unlikely window of the Canadian literary world. It is true that a Crown corporation, the CCC, negotiated the contract with the Saudis. But they were doing so on behalf of a publicly-traded corporation, General Dynamics—which can't afford to turn down such a colossal order—and the hundreds of Canadian companies in the LAV supply chain, none of which has chosen to refuse a subcontract on the deal of a generation. It's the same reason Canadian poets can't afford to withdraw their support for the Griffin Prize. But each of those Canadian firms agreed to make their portion of these weapons of war, and each of those vampires, as Ms Atwood calls them, must bear the onus of the blood they draw. No one touched by the Armoured Brigades Program can afford the luxury of exercising her conscience, not even the poets. It falls upon the back of Raif Badawi to bear the weight of our prosperity.

I realized a few days after Ms Atwood got back to me what

made her responses especially odd and unsettling. Her most famous book, *The Handmaid's Tale*, is set in the fictional Republic of Gilead, a theocratic military dictatorship where women are the chattel of a fundamentalist ruling class and free thought is violently suppressed. Their society's only hope is an underground resistance called the May Day, who carry the torch of liberalism, feminism, and freedom, on pain of death. Raif Badawi is the May Day, and Canadian literature looks on, free to imagine Gilead even as we arm it.

Why poetry? Mr Griffin asks himself the question in his TED Talk. Of all the things he could invest his time and fortune in, why poetry? It has to do with those early evenings in the Griffin family home, memorizing and reciting poems with his father. Yes, the elder Griffin would read poems to his young son, but poetry was more than just cultured entertainment. Growing up, when a young Scott Griffin misbehaved, his father made him memorize a poem, and recite it in front of the family. 'I was back then what you call a difficult child,' Mr Griffin said, 'so I learned a lot of poetry.' As a boy, poems were Mr Griffin's punishment, his penance, their coiled stanzas absorbing the shocks of his transgressions.

'We are in a state of waiting,' Ensaf Haidar says. I spoke to Raif Badawi's wife, through an Arabic translator, on a Saturday. It was more convenient for me to talk on Friday, but Fridays aren't good for her. As we spoke, she'd get distracted by her three young daughters, who were in tow with her as she fit me in between errands in Sherbooke, Quebec.

They met by accident. Raif Badawi dialled the wrong

number, and she answered. 'We spoke,' she said, 'and things developed from there.' He had already been publishing his essays when they met, and had been harassed by Saudi authorities. She married him anyway. 'We believed so much in freedom of speech,' she said, 'that even though we knew that we were risking our lives, we were not afraid.' When the Saudis revoked Mr Badawi's ability to leave the country, Ensaf and their three girls fled to Lebanon. Now she lives with us; we are her asylum.

But on Fridays she waits. If the telephone rings, it could be news that the floggings have resumed—or worse. After Mr Badawi's first beating, in a sickening irony, his jailors deemed him too injured to receive his second. But since, the floggings have continued to be stayed only because of the pressure that the world's writers have applied to the Saudis by reporting about his plight. 'It gives me relief that the world is with us,' Ensaf says. A wave of shame washes over me on behalf of my peers, we happy few, 'the unacknowledged legislators of the world'.

ACKNOWLEDGEMENTS

Thanks to the magazines, newspapers and websites that first published these pieces (and to their editors): the *National Post*, *Poetry*, *All Lit Up*, CBC, *Canadaland*, *The Walrus* and *Slate*. Thanks, too, to the Department of Portuguese and Brazilian Studies at the University of Toronto for the occasion—as if I needed one—to appreciate Ricardo Sternberg. To Ange Mlinko and Gwyneth Lewis, for permission to reprint our conversation from *Poetry*. Special thanks are due to Mark Medley, who let me write a poetry column in the *National Post* for five years, where a lot of these pieces first appeared. That was fun.

Thanks to the Ontario Arts Council, for crucial funding.

Extra warm thanks to Ian Brown, Victor Dwyer, Charlotte Gill and everyone else in the Banff Centre Literary Journalism program for believing in 'The Shock Absorber'.

This book, as with everything else, would have been impossible without the people I love: Mom, Dad, Beb, Jeff, Josh, Sandy, Suzannah and Laura. And thanks to the two who taught me to strike anywhere: Carmine Starnino and Jason Guriel.

ABOUT THE AUTHOR

Michael Lista is an acclaimed poet, editor, critic, and non-fiction writer. He is the author of two collections of poetry: *Bloom* (House of Anansi, 2010) and *The Scarborough* (Signal Editions, 2014). He served as poetry editor of *The Walrus* and as poetry columnist for *The National Post*. His non-fiction appears in *The Atlantic*, *Slate*, *The Walrus* and *Toronto Life*. Lista is the co-founder of *Partisan Magazine*. He lives in Toronto.